Rebecca Eckler

How to Raise a Boyfriend*

Or Any Other Clueless Guy in Your Life

DOUBLEDAY CANADA

Doubleday Canada and colophon are registered trademarks

Library and Archives Canada Cataloguing in Publication

Eckler, Rebecca
How to raise a boyfriend or any other clueless man
in your life for that matter / Rebecca Eckler.

ISBN 978-0-385-67048-7

1. Man-woman relationships—Humor.
2. Etiquette—Humor. I. Title.

HQ801.E35 2011   646.7'70207   C2010-905254-4

Printed and bound in the USA

Published in Canada by Doubleday Canada,
a division of Random House of Canada Limited

Visit Random House of Canada Limited's website: www.randomhouse.ca

10 9 8 7 6 5 4 3 2 1

For all the gals out there who have been there, done that! You are not alone. I thank you for making me feel not so alone either. But mostly, this book is for the constant love of my life, my daughter, Rowan. May she learn from my mistakes and live, as they say in fairytale land, "happily ever after."

Contents

PART 4: **ATTITUDE/EFFORT** 139

PART 5: **I KNOW THIS IS THE WAY YOU ARE** 173

There are always THREE sides when it comes to relationship arguments and stories. There's His side of the story. There's Her side of the story. And then there's the actual truth. The stories and anecdotes in this book are my truths and other women's truths. And though I did have a fleeting thought (or two) that AT LEAST I got material for a book from clueless ex-boyfriends, this is not payback. But if you're one of my exes and disagree with everything I have said about you, and are saying to yourself, "That is *so* not what happened!" then go out and get your own book deal. Call it *How to Raise a Girlfriend.* But for now, this is my book and these are my truths, and this is called *How to Raise a Boyfriend.* Suck it up.

Dear ~~Parents of My Daughter's Potential Suitors,~~
Dear ~~Parents of Any Young Lady or Man,~~
Dear Any Dumb-ass Guy Thinking About Dating Me,

As I write, I think about my six-year-old—specifically her future, specifically her future with men. She believes that the tooth fairy exists, and that her stuffed animals talk. She wants to be a ballerina/Olympic medallist/doctor. She rarely, if ever, is sad. *Even* when it comes to *the opposite sex,* she's full of optimism. She plans to marry a five-year-old named Owen because his name rhymes with hers (Rowan). But sadly, one day my daughter is going to grow up, realize that I'm the tooth fairy and her stuffies can't talk, and start dating for real. Dating! Being in a relationship! Marriage! Talk about a reality check!!!
So please hear me out. One day, my daughter may *date* your son, may be in a *relationship* with your offspring. (You and me? We could be in-laws! That could be fun, right?) My six-year-old is going to realize that rhyming names is not enough for a lasting, healthy, happy relationship.

Maybe it's because I am a single mother, or *especially* because I am a single mother, that I see the lack of civility and common courtesy out there with the men I date. I see my married friends and notice how their husbands treat them. I listen to stories of what my friends put up with in their relationships. I ask my friends, "And are these men going to be role models for your children, who one day may date my little girl?" And, "How can you be married to, let alone live with, a guy like that?"

Like my girlfriends, I'm not totally innocent. I *allow* the men in my life to get away with things I'd *never* let my six-year-old get away with. Ever. Aside from yelling at the men in my life, I really don't know how to let them know that their behaviour is unacceptable. I'm as clueless as my boyfriends are.

This is *not* a "poor me, I'm single" rant. I've rarely had periods of singleness. (Perhaps my standards are a lot lower than yours. In fact, they probably are, which is why I'm writing this damn book!) And I truly have loved all my boyfriends. It's just that while I loved them, their behaviours always ended up annoying me. Their actions (or lack of actions) were not just "eye-rolling" annoyances either. Their habits, the lack of civility and common courtesy, annoyed me to the point that I wanted to pull my hair and scream, "HOW DID YOU END UP LIKE THIS? WHAT IS WRONG WITH YOU?" Of course, I never did.

Because my boyfriends ended up annoying me so much, I started to *hate* them. And when you start to hate the man you're dating, or are, God forbid, married to . . . well, let's just say it's not good. It's so, so not good. After the first couple of dates, if a guy doesn't call when he says he will or is always late, perhaps he isn't worthy. But you're not going to ditch a guy you're married to or living with if he doesn't call you back at the exact moment he says he will. If he's always late, is that a marriage-breaker? Not really. It just doesn't work that way. And my boyfriends WERE INTO ME, even if they were completely clueless. They really, really did LOVE me. I have proof!

The following is from a poem one of them wrote for me (hand-written . . . on paper!). It's sweet, so I kept it. (Plus, he could become totally famous one day.)

I love that I met you
I can't live without you
Even when I'm apart from you
I am a part of you.

See? How sweet is that? Another boyfriend wrote me the following text—one of many he sent, unsolicited, during the course of our relationship:

You are the best present to ever come into my life.

So they were INTO ME. But I had a hard time staying INTO THEM! While my boyfriends could be sweet and lovely in some (and often many) ways, they were just so bad and clueless in many, many other ways. If you're married or in a long-term relationship, I'm sure you know what I'm talking about.

Over the course of a week, a few things happened that led to the idea of this book. First, I went grocery shopping. I had a boyfriend. (Yay!) We were at the stage where he was spending enough time at my house that I wanted him to be comfortable (and not hungry). Not only did I have someone to go to the movies with, someone to have dinner with, someone to have sex with, but I also had someone to go grocery shopping with! I believed going grocery shopping with the man I loved would be fun. You can't get more domesticated than grocery shopping with someone, right? But I realized, while grocery shopping, that if something drastic didn't change (with him), our relationship was going to expire before the carton of 1 percent milk. Yes, the boyfriend who wrote, "I can't live without you," suddenly wanted to ditch me. And I don't mean for someone else. (Has anyone out there ever been ditched at a grocery store? Just curious.)

My boyfriend ditched me at the checkout, with the shopping cart so overflowing I could barely push it, because he wanted to go look for a shirt at a nearby clothing store. So what's the big deal, you ask? Well, it hurt my feelings. We had planned this grocery trip *together*. Plus, a number of the items were for him. The lactose-free milk? His! The contact-lens solution? Um, don't remember needing glasses! Did my boyfriend think I would have *fun* unloading the groceries by myself? Did he think I could *carry* them all without his help? Was he expecting me to *pay* for it all? I wondered what was going on in his head. Had he been *thinking* at all? (What was going on in my head was "YOU CAN'T BE SERIOUS LEAVING ME HERE NOW!") What came out of my mouth was "YOU CAN'T BE SERIOUS LEAVING ME HERE NOW?" He looked at me dumbfounded, like "What's the big deal?"

Of course we got into a wicked fight about what I now refer to with friends as the Grocery Store Incident.

So yes, what was the big deal?

Only a few days earlier, my friend's husband had left her *at the airport* before they were about to get on a plane. (Seriously, I'm not making this shit up.) She was going to attend a three-day conference for work, and spouses were invited. My friend's husband *is* into her too. They have a child together and just bought a new house! He will walk with her in public holding her hand. He just wasn't *into* waiting in line to check luggage. When he saw the long line, he announced, as if he were just at Starbucks and giving up on waiting for a coffee, that he couldn't be bothered. La-de-da, he just took a taxi back home. My friend sent me a text saying, "Change of plans." She didn't seem all that mad—possibly because she was going away on business. But it was as if, you know, that was to be expected, and that's just the way her impatient husband is. As if she was just married to a guy who wouldn't stand in a line to go away with her. (Yes, please take a moment to let this sink in. I did.)

I cuddled with my daughter the night of the Grocery Store Incident (still reeling). I couldn't help but think, "Would I want my daughter to be in a relationship with someone who leaves her to unload, pay for, and carry all the groceries?" And, "Would I want my daughter to be married to a man who ditches her at the airport because of a line?" The answer was no! No! NO! And then something really telling happened . . .

I dropped my daughter off at school the following morning. To get to her classroom, parents must take their children on an elevator. I stood at the back, assuming I would be the last one off. But that wasn't to be.

"After you," announced a smartly dressed male, holding the elevator door open.

I told him that it was okay, that he should get off before me.

"No," he repeated, sweetly and persuasively. "After you!"

I thanked this smartly dressed male, walked out, and thought, "What a charming gentleman!"

Except that he wasn't a *man* at all! He was a *six-year-old*! He was in my daughter's *grade one* class! That is the type of "man" I want my daughter to date one day. Heck, it's the type of man I want to be in a relationship with!

I wondered how it was that a male who had been on this planet for approximately 2,190 days and didn't know how to tell time knew to hold open the elevator for me and let me off first. Just the week before, I had to remind my forty-year-old boyfriend (who has been on this planet for almost 15,000 days) how I hated it when he ran across busy streets, leaving me to fend for myself on the other side or possibly to DIE getting hit by a car if I tried to keep up with him. How was it that a six-year-old had more manners than any man I've dated over the age of thirty?

Later that afternoon, I had an appointment for a Brazilian bikini wax with Helena, my happily married, and very witty, aesthetician. Like most of her clientele, I pour out my relationship woes to Helena. I told her about the Grocery Store Incident. She didn't seem all that shocked.

"All men need to be told what to do," she stated, ripping my hair out.

"But I *already* have a child," I moaned between groans. "I don't have the time or energy to also tell a GROWN MAN what to do and how to behave! My six-year-old has more manners and is more courteous than my boyfriend!"

This, my dear readers, is when I had an *epiphany*. I realized what I should have been doing for years. My married friends who complain about their husbands' thoughtlessness and my girlfriends who moan about their boyfriends' cluelessness should be attempting the same thing!

"OH! MY! GOD!" I screamed to Helena. "I NEED TO RAISE A BOYFRIEND!"

"Yes, honey," she said. "You do."

It made perfect sense! I don't, after all, just get rid of my daughter when she annoys me, misbehaves, or doesn't answer my questions. I don't break up with my child when she whines, eats with her mouth open, or needs to be reminded to brush her teeth. I teach her. I *raise* her to be a better person—a person who knows right from wrong!

In what seemed a sign that God had watched my epiphany at Helena's (and agreed with it), I received my daughter's mid-term report card in the mail a couple of days later. Her report card explained how the teachers "graded" the students.

A: *Indicates consistent achievement at an exceptionally high level.*

B: *Indicates consistent achievement at the expected level.*

C: *Indicates that some progress is being made, and that the student still requires assistance.*

D: *Indicates that little or no progress is being made, and that the student is experiencing significant difficulty and requires assistance.*

Well, dear readers, I ask you: What grade would you give your boyfriend today, when he didn't return your third text? What letter would you give your husband on your last anniversary, when you didn't even get a card? What letter do you want any potential boyfriend to have in a relationship? My daughter got mostly B's, which "indicates consistent achievement at the expected level." (So I must be doing something right!)

But if I were to grade my boyfriend over the past few months, based on his attitudes/efforts/social and physical sciences, I would *have* to give him a C or maybe even a D, which indicates that he is making "little or no progress," and that he "is experiencing significant difficulty and requires assistance." He wasn't doing very well *at all* on the Relationship Report Card scale of things, that's for sure. I wondered if I could get him a tutor. I wondered if I had a special needs boyfriend.

But this book isn't just about men who are clueless. It turns out we women are equally clueless in raising them and telling them what we need or would like from them. While I easily demand that my daughter say please and thank you and clean up after herself, I can't bring myself to tell the men in my life to say the "magic words" or clean up their shit. My daughter tells me she loves me all the time, but my friends' husbands don't even compliment them. So do we just ditch our men for their cluelessness? I don't think so, because if we did, we'd all be single . . . FOREVER.

No, we need to "raise" them like they are our children, but without acting like their mothers.

I figure if I can raise my daughter—a smart and sensitive, kind and generous, thoughtful and polite little girl—certainly I can raise a boyfriend too. So please, take out your highlighters, get your sticky notes, and put on your marking cap, because we're on this journey together. With advice from Freud, my therapist (who charges $200 an hour, which makes this book worth thousands of dollars!), and Helena, my witty aesthetician (who constantly hears women's complaints); guest appearances from my exes (yes, I did call them to figure out why they are so clueless); and a lot of stories from women who clearly need to *raise* their partners, we are going to get the men in our lives to achieve "at an exceptionally high level." Or at least "at the expected level."

We are going to raise them, if not for women in relationships who are sick and tired of getting annoyed at and being disappointed with their men, or for me (who is sick and tired of getting annoyed at and being disappointed with my boyfriends), then please, for my beautiful, brown-eyed six-year-old daughter, who will one day enter the Dating World. She deserves the best, as do your children or future offspring. Like I said, if I can raise a child on my own, certainly I can raise a boyfriend.

xo

Rebecca

P.S. Grocery shopping isn't more fun with a man, even if you love him, even if he doesn't ditch you at the checkout. It's still a chore. It still sucks.

PART ONE

Language Arts

Listening Skills/Oral Expression/Speaking Clearly

Before a marriage, a man declares
that he would lay down his life
to serve you; after a marriage,
he won't even lay down his newspaper
to talk to you.
HELEN ROWLAND

No one is listening until you fart.
AUTHOR UNKNOWN

CHAPTER ONE

Why Is It So Hard for Men to Answer a Damn Question?

ommunication, according to every single article or book on relationships ever written, is the key to a healthy, lasting relationship.
I'd like these "experts" to try to be in relationships with some of
the men I have been with and see how long they'd last. I dare
them! They wouldn't last a second. Communication, after all, is a *two*-way
street. One man I was in a relationship with loved to talk. He loved to talk so
much, I told him on more than one occasion that he was in the wrong profes-
sion and should have been a professor, because then he'd have uninterrupted
hours with an audience required to listen to his rants. This man and I could
waste *hours* together talking about nothing at all, which was fun. (We were
both procrastinators.) He was also one of the smartest people I had ever met,
which is why I was so attracted to him. Except, that is, when it came to
answering basic questions. When it came to answering basic questions, this
man was probably one of the stupidest people I had ever met. Sometimes,
our phone conversations were so painful, I honestly would have rather got
naked, covered myself in honey, and lay on an anthill. Getting answers from
him for very simple questions was *brutal*. This is how our conversations
would typically go:

ME: So what did you get up to last night?
HIM: Oh, I went out.
ME: Oh, you went out. Where did you go?
HIM: Just to a couple of places.
ME: Oh, a couple of places? Which places?

HIM: Just to a couple of bars.

ME: Which bars?

HIM: Just a couple of bars downtown.

ME: Who with?

HIM: Just a couple of friends.

ME: Which friends?

HIM: Just [fill in best friend's name]. And a couple of other people
joined us.

ME: Who were the people?

HIM: Just random people.

ME: So did you have fun?

HIM: It was fine.

ME: Okay, then [silently wanting to pull out his fingernails, or mine,
one by one].

Yes, even I can see that from my questions, I look like a royal nag
or jealous bitch. The truth is, I didn't really care who he went out with or
where he went. I was not jealous. I was making conversation. And I *did* care
that while he was able to recite the entire history of every single war to
ever take place, he was not able to answer the most simple of questions.
(Okay, I'll admit I was 5 percent asking because I can be a royal nag and
jealous bitch. But 95 percent of me was asking because I was genuinely
interested in what he got up to. I really was attempting what they call
"making conversation.") And if you are wondering, he wasn't the cheating
type. He had the highest moral standards, so he wasn't being sketchy with
his cagey answers. That's just the way he was. So I ask you, why couldn't
my boyfriend answer the question, "What did you get up to last night?"
How much *easier* would it be when any gal asks her man, "What did you
get up to last night?" for him to answer, "I went to the Fox and Firkin with
Jim and Bob, and we talked about sports and politics. We had a nice time"?
(Even nicer if he added, "I thought about you the entire time." But let's not
push it.) Why do men turn us into investigators?

Many of my good friends go through the same experiences with their spouses. One friend says of her husband: "I tell him my every move. But he won't answer any of my questions when he comes home after a night out. I'm really just making conversation. I'm not checking in." (And, my friends, unlike me, she's really not the jealous type at all. She really is trying to make conversation with her husband.)

Another friend loves when her husband tries to pull the whole "What did you say?" trick after she asks him a question. "I'll say, 'So where did you go last night after work?' And he'll immediately answer, 'What did you say?' as if it's instinctual. I know he *heard* me. But it's like he's buying time to come up with something, even if he is totally innocent. It's like he just can't help but say that." Another girlfriend never gets straight answers from her husband of ten years. She has finally given up asking. "I just read his e-mails instead," she admits. See? This is not good. We women don't want to have to break into your e-mails just because you can't bring yourself to tell us what you did last night. You don't want us to be *that* woman either, do you?

In fact, sadly, most girlfriends don't seem to fare well in the basic communication department, *especially* when their partners come home from work. When one of my friends asks, "So how was your day?" when her husband arrives home, he actually grunts. (Which makes me feel slightly better about hearing, "Just went out." At least I get *words* from my boyfriend, if only three of them.)

Some of my married friends are lucky if they get a "Fine" from their husbands when they ask how their day was. Then their husbands race away from them as quickly as possible to lounge in front of the television or to work in their home offices. One of my

I'm not your mother! Don't you remember answering your mother's questions when you were seventeen like this: "I'm going out . . . With friends . . . You don't know them . . . I'm not sure where we're going." Yeah, I was like that. (Sorry, Mom.) But guess what? We're not seventeen, and I'm definitely not my boyfriend's mother. So don't make me act like I am.

friends and her husband got into a fight one day over his "non-answers" to her "How was your day?" question. He screamed at my friend for ten minutes about how he "talks ALL day at work," and how he "doesn't want to answer any questions." Hello? My friend wasn't asking QUESTIONS (plural), she was asking one question: "How was your day?" Like me asking my boyfriend about his nights out, my girlfriend asks her husband how his day was because she truly does care to hear the answer. She truly does care how his day was. In the time he spent yelling at my friend that he didn't feel like answering questions, he could have just as easily said, "It was a long day. Lots of meetings."

If I were to grade my boyfriend and my friends' husbands when it came to answering basic questions, they'd *so* get a D on the Relationship Report Card.

No matter how many times I screamed, "Why don't you just answer the damn question?" my boyfriend just couldn't do it. Yes, he needed to be in a remedial boyfriend class. But what could I do? Clearly, yelling at him didn't work.

 ## I JUST SAVED YOU $200 AND FORTY-FIVE MINUTES OF YOUR TIME (TOTAL: $200)

"Freud" is my therapist, and I see him twice a month. His name is not really Freud, but that's what I like to call him. (Not to his face. Just to my friends.) He's a psychologist and knows me better than anyone. He charges $200 for a forty-five-minute appointment. He's sometimes worth the $200. Sometimes he is not. But the fact is, he deals with couples—both women and men complaining about each other in his office five days a week, eight hours a day—and has for more than twenty years. He must know something about what makes relationships work because he probably has heard it all.

I told Freud how my boyfriend, though he loved to talk about everything, had problems answering basic questions, which pissed me off. Freud said that if your man is being "evasive," or giving only one-word answers, you need to be honest with him and say, "You sound evasive. And when you sound like that, it makes me feel mistrustful. And I'm interested in having an open, honest relationship." He explained that for many men, being evasive (and sounding cagey) is a "control thing." Men, he explained, feel that their wives or girlfriends don't have "the right to know every single detail." So we women have to be honest with them. But also, Freud said, we should not come down so hard on ourselves for *wanting* to know answers. "When women don't get straight answers, they assume the worst," he said. He is right. Not only did it piss me off to not get direct and open answers from my boyfriend, but also I assumed the worst, even though he was trust-worthy. (As does my married friend, who checks her husband's e-mails.) Freud said that it's human nature for women to feel that way, which means I'm *normal* to get pissed off at evasive answers. (Yay!)

GUEST APPEARANCE FROM A REAL-LIFE EX OF MINE!

Now, since it takes two to tango in a relationship, I decided to go back to some of my exes—the ones who will still take my phone calls—to ask what was going through their heads when I came down hard on them for certain things. (Actually, I have pretty good relationships with my exes, in the sense that because I'm no longer with them, they don't annoy me so much.) I think it's important for women to hear the men's side of things, even if the men's side is fucking dumb. I figure we can learn something from hearing them out and learning how their brains work. At least that's what I hope. So I asked my ex-boyfriend, the one who always sounded so cagey when I asked him about his nights out, why he never answered my questions and made me work so *hard* to get answers. "I just felt it was none of your business. It made me feel claustrophobic and reminded me that my status was no longer one of independence. It made me feel like a lion in a cage," he ranted. "For men, after a night out, it's done. It's like waking up after a party and seeing a little bit of beer left in a bottle. You wouldn't drink it because you know it's old and tastes like shit. That's what it's kind of like to be asked the question 'What did you get up to last night?' It's done. It's over. I'm not thinking about what I did last night anymore. Plus, I've learned that whenever a girl asks that question, there's an alternative purpose. No matter how innocent their question is, women are waiting to hear something in our tone. They're waiting for us to trip up. That's all they're really listening for—not what we did but our tone. And my married guy friends? Well, if they have the 'night off' from their kids, there's always a bit of resentment from their wives. So don't ask us what we did last night. We know it's a loaded question. A better way of posing it would be, 'Did you have fun?' Or better yet, just let it go and don't ask us at all." (Is it just me or does he sound bitter to you?)

A Word from a Grade-A Husband . . .

Now, I have exactly *one* married friend who is completely happy with her husband. She *never* complains about him. Her husband should be the poster boy for good husbands/boyfriends EVERYWHERE. He is not whipped. He is just a good guy who loves his wife, his family, and his life. I "borrowed" him because I wanted to know what a man who *has* been raised thinks about the problems I and my girlfriends run into with our not fully raised, C-graded men. "Guys don't really like to talk, but men need to realize that there's a small amount of maintenance in a relationship that is easy. Answering the question 'How was your day?' is easy," he says.

WISE WORDS FROM HELENA. She Does My Brazilian Bikini Waxes. She Knows, Hears, and Sees It All!
"Men don't answer basic questions because their baskets are always empty. We should just let it go. But we don't. We're women!" she says.

CLEVER TACTICS/ADVICE ON RAISING YOUR MAN TO ACHIEVE AT OR ABOVE THE EXPECTED LEVEL

*(It would be nice to have them at an "exceptionally high level,"
but let's try for "the expected level" to start with.)*

1. Do not be negative when asking your boyfriend/husband what he did last night. Try your very best to tame your tone so it doesn't sound like you are interrogating him or resent him for going out. Give him time to wake up, or unwind after getting home from work, before you start asking questions. He'll be less grumpy.

2. Talk to him like you're talking to a friend. "Last night I was on the phone with Sheri and we talked about her job, and then I watched a re-run of *Entourage.* What did you do?" Pretend your husband/boyfriend is your best friend and you're just catching up. You're a woman! I know you can act.

3. Joke that you're not his mother. You don't care what kind of trouble he got up to. Joke that you want to live vicariously through him.

4. If you are the type who is strong enough not to ask, maybe just don't ask. And maybe he'll offer it up.

5. Do not look at his BlackBerry for answers. It will just make you feel worse. (Trust me. I've been there.)

6. If you do look at his BlackBerry, do not say anything.

7. Play the "If the tables were turned" game next time you go out. Give *him* one-word answers and then ask him how it feels.

CHAPTER TWO

Pick Up Your Phone and Return My Texts

Some people care too much. I think it's called love.

WINNIE THE POOH

I'm an anxious person by nature. Possibly this is because I'm a mother and am constantly concerned about my daughter. I pretty much know where she is every second of the day, and I know exactly where to reach her at all times. But possibly, I'm just an anxious person by nature. Being anxious, I want to know that my boyfriends are okay. I want my boyfriends to check in with me. Okay? I said it. I admit it. I WANT MY BOYFRIENDS TO CHECK IN WITH ME. Really, what's so wrong with that? Doesn't that mean I care? My boyfriends don't seem to get that I'm not "keeping tabs" when I expect them to call me. I. Just. Want. A. Check-in. Or three. Maybe four. Partly, it's because of how I was raised. Every time I get on a plane, for example, I call my parents before takeoff and also as soon as I land. When my daughter becomes old enough to travel alone, you can bet your ass I'm going to instill this rule. If she has a sleepover, you can bet your ass I check in before bedtime, and I also check in first thing in the morning. I'm not "keeping tabs." I just care!

Men, unfortunately, view women who ask them to "check in" as nags. I, apparently, made the *grave* mistake one night of asking my boyfriend to e-mail me when he got home after his night out. I didn't think this was such a big deal. How easy is it to send an e-mail saying, "Just got home. Hope you're sleeping well. Speak tomorrow. xo"? It's *so* easy. (I know because I just typed that sentence and it took seven SECONDS.)

Of course, my boyfriend didn't e-mail me. Of course, I got pissed off. Of course, we fought about it. When I asked, "Why didn't you e-mail last night?" his response was "I spent the day with you. What's the big deal? You were sleeping anyway." Yes, what *was* the big deal? Well, for one, it would have been nice to wake up to an e-mail from my boyfriend. Two, I wanted to know that he was alive. Three, I had asked for an e-mail that takes only seven seconds to type out, so it hurt my feelings that he wouldn't spend *seven seconds* typing, even after I specifically asked.

"It drives me crazy," my married friend says about checking in on her husband. "I'll leave him message after message, asking where he is or what he's up to. When I ask him why he didn't return any of my messages, he'll say, 'I was out with the boys.'" My friend's issue with her husband's explanation is not that he was "out with the boys." She's not a jealous, insecure person. It's just that when she's out with him, he'll always pick up the phone for "the boys." "So what?" she asks, rightfully so. "He'll be with me and it's okay to pick up for 'the boys,' but when he's with 'the boys,' it's not okay for him to pick up for me? I don't think that's very nice. I think it's rude. I'm his wife! We're supposed to check in with each other."

Sometimes men will go in the opposite direction and check in with their wives too often. "My husband will call me twelve times a day," says an acquaintance. "When he can't reach me, it's like a five-alarm fire. I'm like, 'I didn't pick up the phone because I was out eating with a friend.'" But the problem is not that he calls her so often. For those of us who don't get check-in phone calls, it sounds pretty *delicious* that her husband wants to talk to her throughout the day. But strangely, that's not it. "I'm like, 'Okay, you call me and want to talk to me all day. But the minute you get home, you have nothing to say to me,'" she moans.

Another friend of mine says she used to e-mail her husband during the day to ask him questions about their kids or something house- or bill-related. "He would never e-mail me back. Never. But if I e-mailed him asking him what he wanted for dinner, I'd get a response in two seconds," she says.

So how much is too much when it comes to checking in? When are your expectations too high? I once was in a relationship where—who knew?—I called my boyfriend *too* much. Calling the man in your life too much or not often enough is relative, I learned. Since I work out of my house, like most of my friends, we phone and e-mail and check in with each other all day long. My best girlfriend calls me sometimes twelve times a day. I call her sometimes fourteen times a day. But when you are in a relationship with a man who has an actual job in an actual office, the amount of times you can call to check in becomes tricky.

My friend's husband, an investment banker, actually told her, "Do not call me at work. EVER!" after she called him one too many times one day. "That's what he said. He said, 'Do not call me at work. EVER!'" She laughs, while biting her lip and rolling her eyes. She hasn't called him at his office in nine months. Does he call her to check in? "No," she says.

Another friend of mine was told basically the same thing by her hard-working husband. "He had a talk with me that I couldn't bother him with every little detail going on, and that I should only call if there was an emergency." Guess what happened? My friend got bitten by a rat in her backyard. (I'm not making this shit up!) "I knew I had to go to the hospital, but I was so scared to call him because I had no idea if this was a big deal or not," she says. "We had literally just had the chat about me calling too much a day earlier. So I didn't call. I didn't want to seem like I couldn't handle it on my own. Was getting bitten by a rat an emergency? I had no idea. And also, I *did* want to punish him a little. I mean, I was bitten by a *rat* and had to go to the hospital. I wanted him to feel badly about telling me not to call him so much. I wanted him to feel guilty that I had to go to the hospital on my own, all because he told me not to call him so much." He did feel guilty, and now she's back to calling him all the time. "Again, he just told me the other day that I should only call him when there's an emergency."

I Just Saved You $200 and Forty-five Minutes of Your Time (Total: $400)

I tell Freud that I don't know how often to check in with my boyfriends. Frankly, I admit to Freud, if I'm in love with a guy, I can talk to him ten times a day. And I pick up my boyfriends' phone calls whenever they call, so why don't they pick up mine?

"What's enough?" Freud asks. "For some couples, eight times a day is not enough to check in. For other couples, it's way too much. I've had women complain that their partners call them too often."

When I complained to Freud that my workaholic boyfriend didn't check in enough for my liking, he suggested I lightly say something like "I would appreciate it if you called once in a while. I like hearing your voice." Or, "Even if you could just call and say hi for a couple of minutes, that would be great. I like it when you touch base."

And when they do call, we women have to reward them, Freud says. "Like giving them a blow job?" I ask. "Oh, Rebecca," he laughs, shaking his head. "I was thinking more like saying, 'I'm really glad you called.' Or, 'I appreciate that you took a minute out of your day to talk to me.' Or plant a big wet one on their lips when they come home." (Or give them a blow job?)

Still, I wanted an exact number of times it's okay for you to check in with a partner or for a partner to check in with you. I asked Freud, point blank, how many calls/texts/e-mails a woman should, or could, make to her man. (Keep in mind that I have also dated underemployed men who had *a lot* of time to talk on the phone, which was quite different from dating a workaholic with an actual job in an actual office.)

"Rebecca," he said, looking at me with what I think was 90 percent seriousness and 10 percent pity, "just don't be annoying."

I walked out of that appointment thinking, "Did I really just spend $200 so my shrink could tell me not to be *annoying?*" But the truth is, it was sage advice. All I had to do, whenever I wanted to call, was think, "Am I being annoying?" Now, whenever I want to call a man I am in a relationship with,

I hear Freud say, "Rebecca, just don't be annoying." Guess what? I mostly put the phone down now.

GUEST APPEARANCE FROM A
REAL-LIFE EX OF MINE!

I called my ex, the one who didn't respond to my request for a late-night check-in, to ask what he had been thinking by *not* sending the e-mail I requested. He didn't take a beat before launching into his answer. Obviously, he hadn't forgotten the incident either. "What a female is saying when [she wants] you to check in is 'I want to be the last thought on your mind.' It's a really annoying thing. The fastest way to lose a boyfriend is to ask him to check in," he says. (And all along I thought it was by announcing, "Your penis is small.") "Now, if you're on a business trip, that's a different story. Business trips are fraught with issues. Like, 'Did my husband pick up someone at the bar?' So you have to call every night before you go to bed," my ex continues to rant. "Also, when you call, you want to connect with us. It's easier for women to switch gears. For men, it's like pulling us out of the deep lagoon. We can't connect with you right now. If we're working, we can't let anything in emotionally. So if your husband or boyfriend is working and you live together and you're not calling to ask him to bring home a carton of milk, then just fuck off." (Seriously, does this ex sound bitter to you? Would you date him? I did.)

A WORD FROM A GRADE-A HUSBAND . . .

My friend's husband works hard. I asked him what happens when his wife calls to check in on him, which she does about three times a day on average. "There are only two people I'll interrupt my calls for. My wife is one of them, and my mother is the other," he answers simply. (He gets an A, don't you agree?)

WISE WORDS FROM HELENA.

She Does My Brazilian Bikini Waxes. She Knows, Hears, and Sees It All!

"Men never check in enough. And let's be honest, most women
feel more needy some days than others. So fine. Give us the love.
Check in. We're more sensitive. We're women!"

CLEVER TACTICS/ADVICE ON RAISING YOUR MAN TO ACHIEVE AT OR ABOVE THE EXPECTED LEVEL

1. Gently tell your man that you like to hear his voice during the day, if even for one minute. He'll surely be able to find a minute.

2. If he does call, make sure you show your appreciation. When you see him next, give him a kiss (or a BJ), saying you appreciated that he took time out of his day to say hi. He'll learn that if he does check in, he will be rewarded.

3. Remember the Winnie the Pooh quote "Some people care too much. I think it's called love"? Say it with your cutest tone. How can any man not agree with Winnie?

4. Don't be "annoying" with your calls and e-mails. Before you make that second/third/fourth call or send that second/third/fourth e-mail, ask yourself, "Am I being annoying?" If you have to wonder, you probably are about to be annoying. That should stop you.

5. The less you check in, the more he will.

CHAPTER THREE

Magic Words.
Men Did Go to Kindergarten,
Didn't They?

With one look, my daughter knows she ain't getting no straw for her apple juice if she doesn't say please and thank you. In fact, she pretty much gets nothing she asks for unless there's a please first and a thank-you following. She's a quick learner. Because most times when my six-year-old asks for something, she'll say please and thank you. When someone compliments her, she says thank you. When she orders food at a restaurant, she says, "Can I please have french fries?" Why? Because my six-year-old *knows* the Magic Words. How? Because, after *Mama* and *Dada*, usually *please* and *thank you* are the words kids learn next when they are starting to talk. I've raised my daughter to LIVE BY THE MAGIC WORDS. She's knows that USING THE MAGIC WORDS is polite. Whether you have children or not, I'm pretty damn sure that if you haven't been living under a rock your entire life, you know the Magic Words too. Sure, my daughter can't do up her own shoelaces yet, but she's smart enough to know that things *happen* when she uses the Magic Words. So how come men don't know this? Why aren't they as polite as my six-year-old?

I was in a relationship with a man who dressed very well, was very funny, and made a lot of money. I liked him quite a bit. He invited me over to his parents' house for dinner on the night of a major

HOW IT GOES WITH MY SIX-YEAR-OLD . . .

"Mommy, can I have a straw for my milk?" my daughter asks.

"What do you say?" I respond.

"Please can I have a straw?" she'll say.

(I dangle the straw in front of her.)

"Thank you," she responds, smiling sweetly.

Jewish holiday, Passover. Our relationship was very good and moving along smoothly. He wanted me (and my daughter) to be a part of his family on an important night in the Jewish world. (A very big deal.) Make that, our relationship *was* good until he sent me an e-mail the afternoon of that dinner that read, "My parents asked me to bring a shank bone tonight. Can you get one?" "What the hell is a shank bone?" you're probably asking. Well, a shank bone is something that *needs* to be at a Passover dinner. My boyfriend sent me the e-mail at 2 p.m. Dinner was at 6 p.m. Now, let's forget about the short notice for a moment. Let's forget, too, that finding a shank bone ON THE DAY OF PASSOVER is a nearly impossible task, unless you have an "in" with a butcher, which I did not. (Finding a shank bone on the day of Passover is like finding the trendiest toy on Christmas Eve.) No, it was *the way* my boyfriend went about asking me to get a shank bone. Actually, it was the way he *didn't* use the damn Magic Words that got my back up. If he had sent an e-mail that said, "Can you *please* try to find a shank bone? *Thank you* so much," I may have at least attempted to do it. But the fact that he didn't even bother with a please or a thank-you actually made me actively not want to do it at all. Of course, we got into the Shank Bone Argument and our relationship was never the same, and let's just leave it at that. He didn't understand why I didn't just do it. He didn't understand that the Magic Words were important to me. (After that, I realized how rarely he said please or thank you for anything.)

Another man I seriously dated was also seriously bad with the Magic Words. (Let me just remind you that all the men I date are over thirty, some *well* over thirty.) I was out to lunch with a girlfriend, and as we were about to leave, I said, "You know, I think I'll bring a sandwich back for Mike" (not his real name). Mike was waiting for me at my house, and I got all starry-eyed thinking about him as I ordered him his favourite deli sandwich.

"That's so nice of you," my friend said. "You are such a good girlfriend." Was I? Well, I like to think so. It was nice of me, but it wasn't a big deal. I was already at the restaurant. It was just a sandwich. But yes, I *was* a good girlfriend. (I'd give myself an A on the Relationship Report Card, since I was always thinking about Mike and doing thoughtful little things for him.)

Shortly after, I was at home, watching Mike eat the sandwich I had brought back for him. I watched and I waited. I waited and I watched. I waited and I watched as he wolfed down the entire sandwich as if he hadn't eaten in a week. As I waited and I watched, I kept thinking, "He didn't say thank you." He didn't say it when I handed the sandwich to him. He didn't say it while he was eating it. He didn't say it after he had thrown out the wrapper and announced, "That was good!"

I stared at him.

"Why are you looking at me that way? Do I have mustard on my face or something?" he asked. Now, if he had been my daughter, I would have easily said, "What do you say when someone does something nice for you?" In fact, my daughter wouldn't have been eating the sandwich unless she had said thank you as I handed it to her. But I just couldn't bring myself to say to my adult boyfriend, "You know, you never said thank you for the sandwich that I so thoughtfully brought you back. You didn't use THE MAGIC WORDS!" How do you say that to a man in his forties? Why was I letting him get away with something I'd never let my daughter get away with? I just shook my head at him and wondered, "Is he really that clueless?" And, "Is he really for me?" The stars in my eyes started to fade. I stopped going out of my way to do nice things for him too.

Even my long-married friends seemed to have given up on hearing the Magic Words from their spouses. Still, they're constantly annoyed with the fact that they don't get a simple thank-you. My best girlfriend is not only a really good cook, but has also managed to raise three (polite) children. She and her husband still have sex three times a week, so I'd say their relationship is pretty good. However, what is *not* good in their relationship is that he never says thank you to her. "It would be nice," she moans, "if my husband came home from work and, instead of yelling about the toilet that's broken or the toys all over the house, said, 'Thank you for the dinner that took you two hours to make, after picking up all the groceries by yourself.'"

Another friend says that whenever she bought her husband a gift, she never got a thank-you. "He was okay with the 'Pleases,'" she says. "But

'Thank you'? Never. Every single present I got him, all he'd give me was a 'It's not bad.'" She resorted to always saying to him, "A thank-you would be nice!" And her husband would just roll his eyes at her. (He gets a D: Indicates that little or no progress is being made, and that the student is experiencing significant difficulty and requires assistance.)

I Just Saved You $200 and Forty-five Minutes of Your Time (Total: $600)

I asked Freud what is up with men who don't use the Magic Words. After the sandwich incident with Mike, I was pissed, so of course I wasted at least twenty minutes of my time with Freud ranting about it. (Yes, I spent almost $100 complaining about this incident. I try not to think about it.) Freud's answer was simple. "It's a character flaw," he stated as he looked me directly in the eyes. "Well, okay. Great," I thought. So I date guys with "character flaws." And my friends are married to men with "character flaws." So what the HELL do we do about it? "Some people just lack good manners. Some men become complacent. If you're always doing things for them and they never thank you for it, it could be complacency," he added. He suggested that women remind their men, in a POSITIVE WAY, that they should be appreciative. And saying please and thank you is a way of showing your appreciation. I kind of lean to saying, "What are the Magic Words, asshole?" But I suppose I could try to cutely say, "What's the Magic Word?" and leave out the "asshole" part.

WISE WORDS FROM HELENA. She Does My Brazilian Bikini Waxes. She Knows, Hears, and Sees It All!
"Men are just not born with that kind of language. What's with that shit? As men get older, it seems to get worse. You know how they say that when men jerk off, their brain cells go? It's the truth! They forget! And manners is one of the things they forget."

CLEVER TACTICS/ADVICE ON RAISING YOUR MAN TO ACHIEVE AT OR ABOVE THE EXPECTED LEVEL

1. Jokingly suggest he go back to kindergarten. When he says, "Huh?" say, "You forgot the Magic Words."

2. Don't let him get sloppy. I never let my six-year-old get away with not using the Magic Words. If you let it slip once, he will become complacent.

3. Send him to manners class. Or at least suggest that you're thinking of sending him to manners class. He may get it.

4. Tell him you need to feel appreciated. Lie. Say that you have had a bad day, that no one at work appreciates you, and that a little "Please" and "Thank you" from the guy you love goes a long way in making you feel better.

5. Dangle whatever it is you got him in front of him, like I do with my daughter. He'll get the hint that he needs to say please.

CHAPTER FOUR

You Say Nothing and I Say Hello

If the person you are talking to doesn't appear to be listening, be patient.
It may simply be that he has a small piece of fluff in his ear.
WINNIE THE POOH

I have a real issue with proper hellos and goodbyes. When my daughter comes home from school and doesn't say hi, I gently suggest that she do so. She understands that when she sees me, she is expected to be happy, or at least to greet me with a hello. Luckily, she usually does. And I also get a kiss! Also, every morning before she goes to class, I get a big hug and sometimes five kisses on my face.

One man I dated made the most delicious meals for me. He was so talented and skilled in the kitchen (and in the bedroom, but—ahem—that's not important here). He was *not* talented or skilled in any way whatsoever, however, when it came to greeting me on the phone when I called. Which is odd, because he was forty-two years old, and even if he had answered the phone only two times a day for twenty years . . . well, that's a hell of a lot of practice in answering the phone with a proper greeting. The problem was, he always kind of sounded *disappointed* to hear from me. FROM ME! The love of his life! Even my seventy-year-old father has call display, so it's not like my boyfriend didn't know who was calling.

The Dude would answer, if I was lucky, with a "Hey," which was fine. (If a girl says "Fine," you know it's never fine.) However, most of the time he'd answer with a "Yeah?" Which made me feel as if I was bothering him. And also, it made me feel like telling him that if he didn't want to hear from me, then he should just not answer the damn phone. But of course, mostly I'd say sarcastically, "Oh, you sound *really* happy to hear from me!" In fact, I'd rather he not pick up the phone than answer with a "Yeah?" Hearing my boyfriend answer my phone call that way was like hearing him answer with a "What the fuck do you want now?" Of course, once I said, "Oh, you sound *really* happy to hear from me!" my boyfriend's back would immediately get up and usually we'd bicker, because he'd put me in a mood with his so-not-polite greeting.

In person, men sometimes don't greet you any better. One of my friends met her long-time boyfriend for breakfast one morning at a local diner. She arrived earlier than he did and took a seat at a table. He arrived shortly after, saw where she was, walked up to the table, sat down on the chair, and grunted out something that may or may not have been a hello. "There was no kiss or anything," my friend said. "I don't care how hung-over he was. The fact is, it's just so rude!"

No argument from me. A grunt is not a greeting. A grunt is RUDE. But my friend was lucky that she even got a grunt. And when it comes to good-byes? Oh, my. Oh, my.

One of my girlfriends makes amazing banana muffins. That has nothing to do with goodbyes, but I wanted to note how good her banana muffins are because they really are *that* good. One morning I was at her house, eating one of her amazing banana muffins in her kitchen with her and her two children. I often stop by her house in the mornings to say hi before I go to the gym, because I adore her and her children (and her banana muffins). That morning while I was visiting, her husband called out, "Okay, I'm leaving," and then we all heard the front door slam. I didn't even bother hiding my shock. "Seriously? Is that how he leaves every morning?" I asked. "Doesn't he come in and see you and give you even a quick peck on the cheek? Doesn't he say goodbye to your kids?" Even my boyfriend who answered my calls with a "Yeah?" would always say goodbye and give me a kiss.

"Oh," she responded, "he's not going to the office."

"Where's he going?" I asked, confused.

"He's going to New York on business for three days."

Okay, my friends, I practically fell off her kitchen stool when I heard this. "Your husband is going away for THREE DAYS and that's how he says goodbye to you and your kids?" I said, staring at her.

"Oh, I don't even notice it anymore," my friend responded nonchalantly. Then she asked, "Another muffin?"

I was sick at witnessing how her husband said goodbye! I couldn't stomach another muffin. Her man needed some raising and fast. (I'd give her husband a D on the Relationship Report Card. In fact, I'd give him an F.) Seriously, how hard is it to walk into the kitchen and say goodbye? Also, he has two sons who one day could date my daughter. Doesn't he know he's a role model to his children? Doesn't my friend realize that she deserves a proper goodbye when her husband is leaving for three days?

Another friend was in a relationship with a man who always ended his phone calls with her with a "Call me later?" "I was like, 'Dude, why don't you call *me* later?'" she says. Endings of phone calls are a good way of seeing what kind of man you are dating. I lean towards this guy being kind of lazy in the relationship department, and maybe he has a few control issues.

But is it too much to expect that our men greet us with a kiss these days? Is it too much to expect a proper goodbye when your man is leaving for work, let alone leaving town for three days?

Another one of my married friends never gets a hello when her husband comes home from work. And he isn't usually even in a bad mood. She tries to converse with him. "It's like talking to a dead wall," she says. "Even if I would say something like 'We're going here this weekend,' I don't get any sort of response. I swear I have no fucking clue if he heard me or if it registered. I was like, 'USE YOUR WORDS!' Even if he just said, 'Okay,' just say something! Show me that you're actually listening to me."

I Just Saved You $200 and Forty-five Minutes of Your Time (Total: $800)

"Me no likey," I told Freud, describing the boyfriend who answered the phone when I called with a "Yeah?" Freud suggested doing what he has done all throughout his marriage (and he's been married for thirty years). "Use humour," he said. "If your boyfriend or husband answers the phone like that, or comes to meet you and doesn't greet you nicely, say something like 'Oh, I thought I was calling my boyfriend.' Or, 'Oh, I thought I was meeting my husband.'" That way, Freud said, you're sending out the message that you didn't like how he greeted you without actually sounding like you're lecturing him. I guess my friend should have chased her husband and said, "Oh, I thought my husband was leaving for three days." I bet that would have worked too, and she would have got a kiss goodbye. And seriously, doesn't he know how lucky he is? She makes *really* good banana muffins.

A Word from a Grade-A Husband . . .

The Fully Raised Man sees why men are bad at greetings and goodbyes. He explains it like this: "There is all sorts of socializing that doesn't come naturally to many men. Guys don't really greet or say goodbye to other men. If I walk into a room of guy friends, when I say, 'What's up?' it's a rhetorical question. Or if a guy says to you, 'What's up?' you don't actually answer it. So while it doesn't come naturally, I've learned to do it. It's really not a hard thing to learn," he says.

WISE WORDS FROM HELENA.

She Does My Brazilian Bikini Waxes. She Knows, Hears, and Sees It All!

"A lot of my clients complain that their husbands or boyfriends just seem neutral when they see them. I'm sure they are happy to see them, but men are just exhausted when they come home. When my husband seems neutral to see me, I'm just like, 'Yeah, whatever.'"

She also tells me a story of how her husband was leaving to play soccer with his friends and didn't say goodbye. She caught him in their driveway just before he left. "I went outside and said, 'Well, goodbye at least!' But I had hurt my back that day, and when he did come home, he did ask how my back was, so he's not all bad."

(She always mentions something thoughtful her husband does, which is why Helena is a good person and wife.)

CLEVER TACTICS/ADVICE ON RAISING YOUR MAN TO ACHIEVE AT OR ABOVE THE EXPECTED LEVEL

1. Say, "Oh, I thought I was calling my boyfriend," in a joking manner.

2. Say, "Oh, I thought I was meeting my husband," in a joking manner.

3. Over the top say, "Oh, it's so good to see you too!" with a big smile.

4. Say, "I think I got the wrong number. I was calling my boyfriend." Hang up and call back.

5. Maybe you don't really care about how he greets you. Do you?

CHAPTER FIVE

Do You Think I'm Pretty? Do I Look Good? Do You Like My Haircut? Then Why the Fuck Don't You Say So?

———————

I can live for two months on a good compliment.
MARK TWAIN *(And he's not even female . . .)*

I am a woman. Therefore, I like getting compliments. If you are like me (a woman), then you like compliments too, even if (like me) you have a hard time hearing them. I mean, haven't we all been there? Haven't you liked a guy so much that you spent your *entire* day preparing to see him? I have.

In the early stages of a relationship, this is how I am: My new man will be getting back from a business trip. I haven't seen him in three days, so we make plans to get together the night he returns. Am I excited to see him? Have you ever lost the lottery? Do you want to win the lottery? Damn right I'm excited to see him! So the day we are going to reconnect, I get my hair dyed at 10 a.m., which takes almost two hours. Then I rush to see Freud, and of course, I end up talking about the guy. Then I race to Helena to get a bikini, underarm, and leg wax, and maybe a manicure and pedicure too. I race home to take an extra-long shower, put on pretty-smelling body lotion *everywhere*, and try on three outfits, to find the perfect one that shows I haven't spent the last hour picking out what to wear. Basically, in order to physically and emotionally prepare to see the guy I'm really into, I spend my entire day getting ready (and emptying my bank account). So yes, I want a damn compliment (even if I'm uncomfortable hearing it)!

In the early days of a relationship, the honeymoon phase—which never lasts, does it?—the compliments do seem to come flowingly. I get compliments, and a lot of them, at the beginning of the relationship. But then something happens. The compliments become rarer and rarer, and sometimes they stop altogether. They become non-existent. The honeymoon is o-v-e-r. Men, I think, don't realize—or stop realizing—that women *like* compliments. They don't know that a good compliment can get us through a week (or at least a night!). We need compliments like a plant needs water. (Wait! I gotta go water my plant . . . Okay, I'm back.)

Not only do I want compliments for myself from my boyfriends, but also I want compliments for my girlfriends from their partners. My girlfriends deserve to get compliments because they are compliment-worthy and fucking fabulous.

I met one of my good friends, who has been married for five years, and her husband at a bar one night for drinks. I knew she had been working out with a personal trainer, three times a week, for months. After not seeing her for weeks, I noticed immediately the change in her body. She looked toned. She looked fantastic. She looked HOT!

"You look amazing," I told her. "That trainer has done wonders."

Then her husband piped up and said, "You've been seeing a trainer? I didn't know that, did I?"

(I'm not making this shit up. Her husband had no idea.)

It was an uncomfortable moment, my friends, to say the least. Just be happy you weren't the third wheel at that table like I was.

Even if my friend's husband didn't know that she had been seeing a trainer, how could he not have *noticed* that her body was banging like she was twenty-one years old again? My friend looked hurt. Clearly, her husband had not noticed the change, and he also hadn't complimented her banging body in months.

"Don't you think I look good?" she asked him as I pretended to look for my BlackBerry in my purse.

"Yes, you look good," he said.

My friend rolled her eyes and looked disappointed.

I got it. What woman wouldn't get it? Soliciting a compliment is *not* the same as receiving an unsolicited compliment. Like my friend, I also find myself asking boyfriends, "Does my hair look okay?" And, "Do you like this dress?" Really I'm asking, "Do you think I look good?" Or, "Do you think I'm pretty?" And I'm also thinking, "Why the hell aren't you saying anything about how gorgeous I am?"

In a moment I'm not proud of, I actually once asked a boyfriend, "Do you think I'm good-looking?" I didn't get the answer I was expecting, which was "Of course you are! You're gorgeous!" The answer I got was "Why are you asking such a stupid question?" Which made me feel NOT good-looking and STUPID—not the ideal combination for a somewhat insecure woman like me, if you catch my drift. So it now seems that we can't even get solicited compliments from our men. What is going on in this world?

I asked all my friends if their partners ever complimented them. Their answers were so depressing that I wanted to curl up in my bed in a fetal position and never leave. One of my most gorgeous married friends is constantly attending black-tie fundraisers, which means she is constantly doing her hair and makeup and getting into sexy cocktail dresses. She looked stunned when I asked, over a glass of white wine at her house, if her husband ever complimented her. "Him? Never. I'll say, 'How do I look?' And he'll say, 'Yeah, you look good. You always look good.' Sometimes he'll even glance up at me from the television when he says that," she tells me. Jesus.

Is it too much to ask for a compliment that is more than "good"? Is it too much to expect our men to actually look at us?

"The best I can get from him is 'You look cute,' and that's rare," moans another one of my friends. This annoys my friend to no end. "It hurts my feelings when he doesn't compliment me," she says. "Seriously, it really hurts my feelings."

I get it. It hurts my feelings too when I don't get a compliment.

Yes, "cute" *is* something. It's better than "You look fine," I suppose. Or, "You look ugly." Or, "Why are you asking me such a stupid question?" It's better than hearing nothing at all. But generally, women are not trying for "cute." We're adults. We're trying for "sexy." We're trying for "gorgeous."

My friend continues, "I was with my husband at a store the other day, and someone said to me, 'You look amazing. You look gorgeous.' I gave my husband a look. I mean, if some random person can tell me that I look 'amazing' and 'gorgeous,' why can't he ever say it?"

I can go on. And I will.

"I never get compliments," says a married friend. "I would literally come down, having gotten ready to go out to an event, feeling really good about myself. Even my daughter would say, 'You look so pretty, Mommy.' My husband would say nothing. I would ask, 'So do I look okay?' And he'd be like, 'Yeah, you look good.' But I'm *always* the one to say, 'What do you think of this top?' Usually, instead of any compliment, I will get 'Oh, how much did it cost?' Or, 'Oh, you needed a new dress?' Ouch."

Another acquaintance says her husband also never compliments her. She once asked him why he never complimented her and his answer was "If I don't say anything, then you can assume you look good." Gee, thanks, buddy.

And then, of course, there are men who are just plain clueless. They really DO NOT notice. For example, one woman I know, who also never gets compliments from her husband, has been wearing the same shade of purple nail polish for months. (The colour matches her BlackBerry cover.) In fact, she's been wearing the purple shade for six months, to be exact. "Just yesterday, he asked me why I was wearing purple nail polish," she tells me. "I said that I liked it and thought it was cute." Her husband then told her, "I think it's the ugliest colour I've even seen in a nail polish." This woman was truly dumbfounded. "I'd been wearing the same colour for SIX MONTHS!" Her husband really hadn't noticed.

Another friend agrees that some men just don't notice. Hers is one of them. "I do think men know they're missing something. I'll come home and he'll be like, 'Okay, is your hair different? No, you got a tan? Wait, did you get a facial? Something?' I think he just knows that I went somewhere to do some personal upkeep, but he still has no clue what I've done."

Other men who aren't good at giving out compliments are quick to point out flaws. "My husband does compliment me occasionally, but more often he'll say, 'Don't wear that skirt. It's not flattering,'" says another gal pal. One poor woman I know went to a formal event with her husband. The event lasted five hours, and she noticed that her husband was in a rotten mood the entire night. Once they were in a taxi on the way home, she asked him why he was in such a bad mood and if something had happened at work. "His answer was 'No, your dress put me in a bad mood.'" Ouch. Ouch. Ouch.

And then there are men who overly compliment, to the point where none of the words ring true. "My ex-boyfriend's compliments just seemed so fake," said one friend. "He'd be like, 'I see so many sexy women, but you're the sexiest woman I've ever seen. I've never had better sex with anyone.' And he'd go on for ten minutes. It was just so over the top that it was bullshit."

I Just Saved You $200 and Forty-five Minutes of Your Time (Total: $1,000)

"I see women in relationships all the time who don't feel cherished," Freud says when I ask him why men seem to have such issues with compliments. Compliments, it turns out, are a huge deal-breaker in marriages. "The predominant breakdowns of marriage, or infidelity in marriages, take place because people's needs are not being met and the women aren't being made to feel cherished." (OMG. A COMPLIMENT CAN SAVE YOUR RELATIONSHIP! This is from a *professional*!)

GUEST APPEARANCE FROM A
REAL-LIFE EX OF MINE!

I asked one of my serious exes, "Why did you never compliment me?" This was his response: "I want you to imagine me with my best friend. What if I saw him and said, 'Wow, Jon! You look great today! You look awesome today! Did you get your hair cut?' It's insane, right? I was not in the habit of giving compliments. Women compliment other women all the time, but guys are not used to this. Also, most human beings don't like to have to do things when they are required. As soon as you want it, it's human nature to withhold it. Many women are insecure. We realize that it will never end, that our women will never be satisfied. It's like having your favourite food. You can eat it and eat it but still not be satisfied. You start complimenting a woman and it will never end, and you have to do it every day. Fuck that. Anyway, you'd never take compliments. You'd always get so uncomfortable and say you looked like shit, so why should I have bothered?" (Yes, I dated this man . . . for a while. If I were you, I'd stay away.)

A WORD FROM A GRADE-A HUSBAND . . .

"I compliment my wife all the time. I'm amazed how easy it is to light up a girl's face. I'll tell my wife she looks gorgeous, and she'll say, 'Oh, but I don't have any makeup on, and I'm in my trackies.' But still. Not giving a woman a compliment is like finding a ten-dollar bill and not picking it up. It's just too easy to pick it up. Just like it's too easy to give a compliment," he says.

WISE WORDS FROM HELENA.

She Does My Brazilian Bikini Waxes. She Knows, Hears, and Sees It All!

"A lot of my clients who are dating get the compliments from their boyfriends.
But then it becomes serious and it just flies from their minds.
And [the women] practically have to beg. Most of my female clients
always compliment their husbands. I call it 'brain erase.'
Men figure we magically know that we look good. And of course we do. But
when I compliment my husband, why can't he give me the same courtesy?"

CLEVER TACTICS/ADVICE ON RAISING YOUR MAN TO ACHIEVE AT OR ABOVE THE EXPECTED LEVEL

1. Come out of the bathroom or go downstairs and do a sexy pose. Pull out your inner model. That's like asking, "How do I look?" without having to ask the question. Hopefully, your boyfriend won't say, "What the hell are you doing?" He'll say, "You look gorgeous."

2. Do not have a crying spell because he doesn't compliment you. Be direct and say, "It makes me feel good when you notice me all dressed up."

3. Don't use negative words like "You never compliment me." He'll just blank you out.

4. Pull out any trick you have. One of my favourites is to say that I was a really ugly teenager, so I'm insecure and need to be told when I look good. Ha!

5. Reward him with a big kiss (or the promise of a sexual favour later) if he compliments you. I've learned to say, "That's so sweet," and give a big juicy kiss.

6. Don't forget to compliment him when he looks good!

7. Don't be like me. If he compliments you, say thank you.

CHAPTER SIX

Seriously! *They Are Only Three Words:* I LOVE YOU

———

I like not only to be loved, but to be told that I'm loved.
GEORGE ELIOT

My heart always skips a beat whenever my daughter says "I love you." Sometimes, we'll just be sitting watching television and she'll say, "Mommy, I love you," out of the blue. Of course, she always says "I love you" when I say it to her. But she also says it for no reason, completely unexpectedly. I can be driving and she'll be in the back seat.

"Mommy?" she'll ask.

"Yes, baby?"

"I love you," she'll say.

Or we'll be brushing our teeth and she'll say, "Mommy, I love you."

And it so, so, *so* warms my heart. Men, well . . .

What the fuck is up with men and these three words? This is kind of like not getting compliments, but it's even worse. We want to hear, "I love you," but we don't want to have to ask men to say it to us. That's even worse than having to ask for a compliment.

"He'll never say it unless I say it first," a number of women have told me about their partners. One of them even asked her husband why he never tells her he loves her. "He said, basically, that if he doesn't say, 'I *don't* love you,' I should just assume that he loves me. It's kind of like no news is good news," she says.

Great. So do we all have to wait until the day our partners say, "I don't love you," getting nothing in the meanwhile? No news may be good news, but it's so not good enough.

One of my serious boyfriends had no problem saying "I love you"—as long as we had been in a fight and there were tears (mine) and makeup sex. If we weren't fighting, our conversations would go quite differently. I'll take you back to when we first started saying "I love you" to each other. The conversation went like this:

ME: I love you.

HIM: Yeah, yeah.

ME: I just said, "I love you."

HIM: Yeah, yeah.

ME: Oh, for God's sake! What the fuck is your problem? When I say,
    "I love you," you're supposed to say, "I love you too."

HIM: I love you too.

Flash forward to two years later. I was still seeing this man. We would be on the phone, or be together in person, and the conversation would go like this:

ME: I love you.

HIM: Yeah, yeah.

ME: I just said, "I love you."

HIM: Yeah, yeah.

ME: Oh, for God's sake. What the fuck is your problem? When I say,
    "I love you," you're supposed to say, "I love you too."

HIM: I love you too.

Yes, *two years later* he was still saying, "Yeah, Yeah," when I told him, "I love you." (Obviously little or no progress was being made. Obviously, I had a "problem" boyfriend.)

"Yeah, yeah"? Is that really a good response when someone tells you she loves you? Really? I say "I love you" to my friends and family all the time. I said "I love you" just the other day when a perfect stranger helped me pick up my change after it all fell out of my wallet in the middle of the street. In fact, if you do anything remotely kind to me, I'll give you an "I love you." It's not hard for me to say the words, so why is it so hard for the men in my life to say them to me, someone they really *do* love?

I tried for a while not to say "I love you," because I couldn't bear to hear "Yeah, yeah" as a response. I lasted one day. It wouldn't have worked anyway. I'm a woman, and the words just come out of my mouth. I like to say "I love you" when I love you. I like to hear that you love me too. So say it!

GUEST APPEARANCE FROM A REAL-LIFE EX OF MINE!

I asked Mr. Yeah, Yeah, my ex, why he always answered like that when I said, "I love you." Here's what he told me: "Let me ask you: Would you want a guy who was saying 'I love you' to you all the time? Every time you walked in a room or left a room? No, then you'd think we were needy. You'd be totally turned off. In fact, by not saying it, it's a strange sign of respect. You got us. We married you. Or we're in a relationship with you. Think about it. Really? You want us to be [saying], 'I love you. I love you. I love you'?" (Okay, he has a point. It would sound a little needy. I would probably be a little turned off. NOT THAT I EVER GOT TO HEAR IT ENOUGH TO KNOW!)

A WORD FROM A GRADE-A HUSBAND . . .

"I always say it back," says my friend's husband, who is fully raised. "Half of it is good manners and being a good boyfriend or husband. Truthfully, it's not because I'm sensitive or she has me by the balls. It's more like a mathematical time equation. If you don't say it back, you poison the mood. And if she's in a bad mood and just needs to hear 'I love you,' and I don't say it, the night will suck. And why would I want my wife to be in a bad mood?"

CLEVER TACTICS/ADVICE ON RAISING YOUR MAN TO ACHIEVE AT OR ABOVE THE EXPECTED LEVEL

1. Remind yourself that men don't need to hear the words as often. That's not to say they don't need to hear them. Just not *as often* as we do.
2. Tell him you have low self-esteem and you need to hear the words. (It works for me.)
3. Quote George Eliot: "I like not only to be loved, but to be told that I'm loved."
4. Reward, reward, reward when he says it.
5. Say "I heart you" instead. It's the same thing, and maybe he'll think it's cute.

CHAPTER SEVEN

Why Saying Sorry Is as Hard for Men as Asking for Directions

To be happy with a man you must understand him a lot
and love him a little. To be happy with a woman you must
love her a lot and not try to understand her at all.

HELEN ROWLAND

My daughter and I have had this discussion about apologizing numerous times. Sometimes, I explain, even if it was an accident or you didn't mean to hurt someone, you still have to apologize. She's also learned that sometimes an apology, even one offered when she didn't do anything wrong, makes another person feel better. We were at a play date recently with two other children. One of the other children felt left out and started to cry. My daughter, without any pressure from me, said she was sorry to the little boy, just because she felt badly that he was crying. If only men could be as smart and sensitive as my six-year-old. But they're not.

I guess I'll apologize right now for being the type of woman who needs an apology when a man does something wrong in a relationship. Let me repeat: I NEED

HOW IT GOES WITH MY SIX-YEAR-OLD . . .

"But I didn't mean it," my daughter moans, after she accidentally lands on a boy's head coming down a slide at a park.

"Apologize," I demand, even though the little boy did appear out of nowhere.

"I'm sorry," says my daughter to the little boy.

THE APOLOGY. I need to *see* on your face that you are sorry, and I also need to *believe* that you are sorry. The importance of an apology in a relationship cannot be underestimated, in my opinion. In fact, sometimes I think the only people in long, happy relationships are the ones with men who know how to apologize. And I don't mean getting an apology like "Fine. I'm sorry you're feeling that way," which, of course, really means he's not sorry at all. No, I'm talking about the honest-to-goodness, heartfelt apology. My married friends know what I'm talking about. "I'll take the apology from him," says one of my married friends, "if it's sincere. But not if he's like, 'Well, I'm *sorry*, then.'"

Oh, memories. I have had a number of boyfriends who just didn't know when/how/why to apologize. But one truly sticks out.

I had been at the restaurant for thirty minutes, breaking my self-imposed rule that I always leave after twenty. I knew he was about to come any second. My heart would skip a beat every time the front door opened. It's . . . no, it's not him. It's . . . no, it's not him. Finally! It's . . . no, it's not him. I just knew my guy would walk in at any moment. We had a surprise birthday party to get to, and we were definitely running late. So I ordered, because I knew the next time the door opened . . . no, it's not him. I called, but he wasn't picking up. Finally, my phone rang.

"Where are you?" I asked, not bothering to say hello. He was thirty-one minutes late now.

"Where are *you*?" he asked.

Did I just hear him correctly? Was he serious?

"I'm at the restaurant where we said we'd meet half an hour ago," I responded curtly as the waiter placed the food (for two!) on the table. "Where are you?"

"I fell asleep," he said. "I'll be there in ten." (I hate when people say they'll be there in ten. In this city, that's always everyone's standard answer. No matter how far away they really are, you'll hear, "I'll be there in ten!")

He hung up before I could respond. I stared at all the food on the table before me and was no longer hungry. He. Fell. Asleep. HE FELL ASLEEP? HE FUCKING FELL ASLEEP!

I tried to eat a sushi roll, because when a gal orders three dozen maki rolls, two salads, and two miso soups, you can't help but think she was stood up or is not respected enough for her date to show up on time.

Twelve minutes later (not that I was keeping track or anything!), my boyfriend breezed in, took off his jacket, sat down, looked at all the food on the table, and announced, "This looks good."

I looked at him, trying to keep my eyes blank. But surely my sour expression must have given him a tiny clue to how I was really feeling. I didn't say anything. It was awkward. Finally, he said something. He knew I was waiting for some sort of explanation. Points for that!

"I don't know what happened," he explained. "I was just so tired, so I decided to lie down, then I woke up and realized that I had no idea how long I'd been out for. Then I looked at the clock and realized I was late meeting you," he said. (Of course, since I am female, I translated that to mean, "I totally forgot about you.")

I continued to stare at him. I was furious. I wanted the apology. But he was gorgeous. But I was FURIOUS. I wanted the apology. But he was GORGEOUS. I continued to stare at him with an expectant look, which I hoped communicated, loud and clear, "WHERE'S MY APOLOGY?"

Obviously, my expression didn't work. He continued to eat away, occasionally letting out a happy sigh. Quite frankly, I didn't really care that he fell asleep. I get it. Shit happens. But he was very late, and surely I deserved an apology, if not five. I wondered what would have happened if he had been meeting the Queen instead of me. Would he apologize then? What if he had plans with his boss? Wouldn't he apologize to his boss if he were forty-two minutes late?

You'd think that most married men at least would know how important the apology is. But they don't. One of my married friends is convinced that men never like to admit they're wrong, and that's the reason getting an apology out of them is like getting them to ask strangers for directions. They'd rather do anything but.

"My husband completely forgot about our anniversary. He knew he had done something wrong, and he had been making up for it by being extra nice to me and buying me gifts," a friend recently admitted to me. "But it's a week later now and I still haven't heard, 'I'm sorry.'" To her, that would be the best gift (not that she didn't do well with the guilt gifts). In fact, she's so used to not getting an apology and getting guilt gifts instead, she doesn't say anything. "I used to really care that he would never say he was sorry. Now I just take the gifts."

A now separated friend found out that her husband had been cheating on her for years. Finding out their marriage had all been a lie was bad enough, but she still didn't get an apology. "We got into a huge fight about it. And I finally said, 'You know, you've never even apologized.'" Even after she knew she was out of the marriage, even though she knew they were going to get divorced, she still wanted the apology.

Men don't realize that there's a difference between admitting you fucked up and actually apologizing. "My husband totally forgot about coming to see me speak at this conference, and he still hasn't said he's sorry," one friend told me. "He admitted he 'fucked up,' but I never got an actual 'I'm sorry.'" Another friend would sort of, kind of get apologies, which—make no mistake—is not the same as getting an actual apology. "He'd apologize, but always with a qualifier. Like, 'If you hadn't done that, then I wouldn't have done that. So I'm sorry if I did that, but it was only because you did that!'" she said.

Men, in my experience, haven't learned that if they've done something wrong, they should just say, "I'm sorry." It's much cheaper (and easier) than a week of guilt gifts. Plus, the sooner you say, "I'm sorry," the sooner we can say, "I accept your apology," and move on with our lives. We can't forgive you if you don't say sorry. Until, that is, the next time you screw up.

I Just Saved You $200 and Forty-five Minutes of Your Time (Total: $1,200)

I admit to Freud that when a boyfriend does something wrong, or says or does something that hurts my feelings, I'm the type of woman who needs the apology. I can't just let things go, I explain. "I need the 'I'm sorry.' And then I need it again and again," I say.

"Do you need five apologies, or do you just need one really sincere one?" Freud asks.

Hmmm. (He had a point. This is why I pay him the big bucks!)

"I guess I wouldn't need five apologies if I got one *really, really* sincere one," I say. Turns out, I'm normal! (Yay!)

Women, Freud says, can tell when a man is saying "I'm sorry" just to end the conflict and when he really is sorry for his actions. I like Freud today, especially when he adds that even if women get upset for totally unreasonable, ridiculous reasons ("You said you'd call at ten and now it's 10:05 p.m."), a man will apologize if he really loves you. But first, you may have to explain to your man how his actions impacted you and made you feel. "Even if a man doesn't exactly recognize what he's done wrong, he should be sorry that he hurt you if he really loves you." So, gals, speak up! Explain why you are hurt, and maybe you'll get that *one* really sincere apology. (Or five half-hearted ones, which may work for you.)

Guest Appearance from a Real-Life Ex of Mine!

Why was it so hard for one of my exes to say "I'm sorry," even though he knew it would make me feel better? (Because I told him that an apology would make me feel better, even if he didn't purposely do something wrong?) Well, I asked. And this was the answer I got: "Men don't apologize because we're usually right. Men are creatures of justice and rightness. All women want is an apology, but you're wrong! Why do girls always need an apology? Do women apologize all the time? It's such a double standard! And hey, did you ever apologize to me?" (Yes, I tell him, I did!) "Sure, but I'd have to drag it out of you. Sometimes it would take *months* [for you] to say you were wrong. And then sometimes you'd take it back!" (This could be true. Ah, the power of repression!)

A WORD FROM A GRADE-A HUSBAND . . .

"I apologize a lot," he says. "But I know how to do it right. You do have to be careful about your apologies. I've learned not to be excessively apologetic, because it loses its sincerity."

———◆———

CLEVER TACTICS/ADVICE ON RAISING YOUR MAN TO ACHIEVE AT OR ABOVE THE EXPECTED LEVEL

1. Women need to be direct about why they are hurt or what their guy has done wrong. Or else they will *not* get an apology.

2. If the apology seems heartfelt, take it. Don't harp on it. Let it go.

3. Don't make him apologize for EVERYTHING. Pick your battles. If you make him say he's sorry for leaving a dish out, not being home on time, and sleeping in too late, he'll just become resentful.

4. Take the guilt gifts. It is a man's way of showing that he knows he's done something wrong.

5. If you do something wrong, apologize. Make it heartfelt. Maybe he'll follow your lead. Let's face it: we're not perfect either.

CHAPTER EIGHT

How Can You Fall Asleep?
We're Just Starting the Fight!
You Have Another
Three Hours to Go, Buddy!

———

W omen, for the most part, can't go to bed angry. Literally. We can't sleep when we're mad, especially when we're mad at our men. We toss and turn and think about how furious we are. Even if we are so mad we don't want to speak to you, we still want you to try to talk to us. (So we can tell you we don't want to speak to you.) We think of pithy, hurtful things and retorts to say to you, if only you'd speak up. But you're not speaking up . . . because you're fast asleep. Wake up! We will toss and turn to wake you up to make sure you know we're tossing and turning.

I've had some pretty awful words thrown my way in heated late-night arguments. One memorable line was "My heart is just not that into this." (I was like, "Well, your PENIS was into this two hours ago.") Sometimes, men can be clueless when they choose their words, especially mid-fight, late at night. The problem with us women is that we take you at your word, especially mid-fight, late at night. How can I sleep knowing you just said to me, "My heart is not that into this"? Exactly. But he could. He was fast asleep beside me. So I started crying, and maybe I kicked him (okay, I kicked him), which woke him up. "Why are you crying?" he asked, pulling me into a hug. He really didn't know why I was crying. "You just told me your heart wasn't into our relationship," I cried. "It sounded like you were breaking up with me." He explained that he hadn't meant it like that, and that he never used those words. In fact, to this day, he will not admit he used those words. But he did. He did. Trust me, he did.

My married friends, even those who seem perfectly suited for each other, of course fight too. One of my best married friends is still traumatized from a fight she had over a month ago with her husband late at night. Mid-fight, he said to her, "I don't think I'm cut out to be married." My friend, of course, didn't sleep at all that night. She spent the night sobbing in their baby's room, wondering if her husband was going to leave her. The next morning, when her husband woke up, he saw that she was still teary. He asked her, "Why are you so upset still?" "Because you told me that you didn't think you were cut out to be married!" my friend wailed. It turns out he didn't mean it. Or at least he didn't mean it *that way*. He had meant that he felt badly he wasn't making her happy.

Another friend got a "You think you're a good wife just because you make dinner?" during a late-night fight. Let's just say she spent a sleepless night on the couch. Another friend, who routinely had major late-night fights with her husband, said to me, "Are you kidding? We used to be getting divorced every week. That was his line when we'd get into wicked fights at night. Our therapist told us to never use those words again, to wipe them out of our vocabulary."

While doing research for this book, I was talking to a man about late-night fights and asked if he ever got into them with his wife. He looked very sheepish. "I've never told anyone this before," he began. "What? Just tell me!" I begged. "Well, when our sex life becomes almost non-existent, I will push her buttons late at night to start a fight with her. Because I know I will get makeup sex." Dear God. And we thought it was all our fault.

 I JUST SAVED YOU $200 AND FORTY-FIVE MINUTES OF YOUR TIME (TOTAL: $1,400)

"I think that rule is bullshit," says Freud when I ask about the old saying that couples should never go to bed angry. "That's a dangerous misconception." Freud says it's sometimes better just to go to sleep. "The later you stay up arguing, the longer and stupider the fight becomes, because you're adding exhaustion into the fight." I think of all the bad night fights I have had with boyfriends. Freud has a point. The fights *do* become longer. They *do* become stupider as the hours tick by. "Generally," says Freud, "late-night fights never really get resolved. The real conflicts never get resolved. And they will keep popping up." He suggests that instead of living by the "We'll never go to bed angry" rule, couples should live by the "Sleep on it" rule. I do this when it comes to work. If I am angry with someone, and before I send off that nasty e-mail I know I may regret, I go for at least a ten-minute walk. Plus, I've asked all my girlfriends about night fighting, and they all agree that the fights *do* become stupider when they should be sleeping. (So we've all agreed that we're going to start fighting in the morning now.) That's not to say you shouldn't try to make up. "Makeup sex is the best," Freud says. (Yes, I do sometimes pay this man $200 an hour for THE OBVIOUS.)

GUEST APPEARANCE FROM A REAL-LIFE EX OF MINE!

I asked one of my exes how he could always fall asleep when we were fighting. "Women can go on about something for just fucking ever," he ranted. "Which is weird. Because at other times, they can shut down a conversation in two seconds flat. But always at night, they never shut up." (Yup, I dated this guy.)

WISE WORDS FROM HELENA.
She Does My Brazilian Bikini Waxes. She Knows, Hears, and Sees It All!
"My husband better not be falling asleep when we're fighting.
He better let me say my piece first!" she says.

CLEVER TACTICS/ADVICE ON RAISING YOUR MAN TO ACHIEVE AT OR ABOVE THE EXPECTED LEVEL

1. No matter how hard it is, SLEEP ON IT. Fights do become stupider and meaner as the night goes on. You know this.

2. Start the fight in the morning. That way, you have all day to figure it out and argue, and by evening you're over it.

3. Try to be kind and gentle. Keep in mind that you are stressed out, probably about other things, and so is he.

4. Try to give him the benefit of the doubt. Try.

5. Never take anything he says after midnight personally.

———

One of my exes constantly told me that I was "crazy." Seriously, in almost every conversation, he'd say that to me. Listen, I'm not "crazy." I prefer to think of myself as "odd." Crazy people don't know that they're crazy. They don't wonder if they're crazy. They're just crazy. Whenever my boyfriend told me I was crazy, I really would wonder if I was. Which means, technically, I couldn't be crazy. I asked this ex why he always said that to me. His answer: "Because you're crazy! What do you want me to say? I told you that you were crazy because you're fucking crazy! You're nuts, honey! Okay, you're not crazy, but you occasionally did crazy things."

HINT!
Never Say These Words to a Woman!

I just wanted to throw in this little paragraph. I polled all my gal pals, and these are sentences we always hate to hear, and always will. So don't say them to us! EVER!

1. "You're crazy."
2. "You're being paranoid."
3. "Are you PMS-ing?"
4. "I don't want to talk right now."
5. "I know you have your period."
6. "You have it so good."
7. "Maybe you shouldn't eat that." (Or, "Are you really going to eat that?")
8. "Are you really going to wear that?"

TIME FOR THE RELATIONSHIP
REPORT CARD!
(Feel Free to Mail This to Your Guy!)

Does he listen?

A   **B**   **C**   **D**

Does he act or comment appropriately?

A   **B**   **C**   **D**

Does he speak clearly and distinctly?

A   **B**   **C**   **D**

Does he use appropriate vocabulary?

A   **B**   **C**   **D**

Does he use different forms of speech for different purposes?

A   **B**   **C**   **D**

Can he describe ideas and experiences clearly?

A   **B**   **C**   **D**

Comments . . .

PART TWO

Social Development/ Social Sciences

Being Late/Bailing/Whining/PDA and More

A little consideration,
a little thought for others,
makes all the difference.
WINNIE THE POOH

CHAPTER NINE

I'm Here . . .
Where the Hell Are You?

I n this day and age, there's no excuse for being late. Rather, there's no excuse for not telling your partner that you're . . . gonna . . . be . . . late. We all have technological devices that allow us to get in touch with other people *at any time we want*, which men seem to do—except, apparently, when they're going to be late. My best friend, a mother of five (did I mention that she's really busy?), made plans to meet her husband for a "date night" at a restaurant in their neighbourhood. She managed to get the kids and the nanny settled, get dressed in a sexy dress with high heels, and get herself to the restaurant to meet her husband for their reservation at 8:30 p.m. She arrived and didn't see her husband. So she called. He didn't pick up. She texted. She didn't get a response. Finally, after twenty minutes, she decided to call his office line. "You've got to be kidding me," she said to him when he picked up. "You're still there?" Her husband told her he'd be there in ten minutes. They've been married for a decade, so you'd think he'd have figured out by now that his wife is *always* on time and hates it when he's late.

"I had now been waiting for half an hour, after the most stressful day, walking over in these gorgeous red heels and sitting there by myself watching all these other couples. I had nothing to read. I felt like such an idiot," my friend said. When her husband didn't arrive after ten minutes, she called him again and said, "I don't know what the protocol on this is, but should I really have to wait more than thirty minutes for you?" He apologized profusely. Kidding! Of course he didn't apologize profusely. He yelled at her: "Don't get mad at the person who is making the money to take you out for dinner!" She hung up on him. Then he called back and apologized profusely. Of course, by then, her night had been ruined.

A recently divorced friend said her husband was always late. "He knew me. He knew that I'm always on time. It was my biggest pet peeve. I'd be in a taxi already and he'd say, 'I'm going to be thirty minutes late.' I'm like, 'Why couldn't you call me *before* I left the house?'"

Another friend moans about her husband: "Last Saturday, he said he'd be home at 11:30 a.m. He came home at 12:30 p.m." Now, it really doesn't seem all that bad, since she was waiting for him at home, with their newborn, which is better than waiting at a restaurant or some other public place. "It was bad because our baby is only up for three hours. And because he was an hour late, he just lost that time with our son."

This same friend and I had plans to go to a book launch. She called me early that day and left a message saying that something had come up and she may not be on time. She also sent me an e-mail with the same message. And she also texted me. Women do this for each other. We give a lot of notice before being late. We apologize at the very thought that we might be late.

Another friend was waiting for her boyfriend to come over. She had been looking forward to the evening, and they had planned for him to arrive at 8:30 p.m. "Then it was ten o'clock and he still hadn't showed. He shows up at eleven, and I'm like, 'Where the fuck were you?' He got all defensive and we got into a wicked argument. I basically said, 'I'm a human being. And if [I'd known] you were going to be so late, then I would have gone out or made other plans.'" Did she kick him out? No, she let him stay. And she fucked him. Because she wasn't sure how to RAISE HIM.

I Just Saved You $200 and Forty-five Minutes of Your Time (Total: $1,600)

If you're at the beginning of a relationship and your guy is chronically late, Freud asks, "Where's your self-respect?" So for all of you in the early dating stages with a guy who is consistently late, you may want to get the fuck out of the relationship *now*. However, when it comes to someone you're in a serious relationship with, or are married to, it's not as simple as dining and dashing. Are you really going to divorce your husband and the father of your children because he's late meeting you at a restaurant? Are you really going to ditch your boyfriend of two years, who makes you breakfast and listens to you moan and gives you foot massages, because he's always late?

Freud again suggests honesty. (What is up with this guy and honesty? Honestly!) He suggests saying something like "It seems you have a problem with punctuality. And it's kind of a character flaw. You want to be the type of person who is punctual for work and *all* areas of your life, including me. It will make you a better person." And apparently, if you are in a loving relationship, you *do* want to make your partner a better person. Not only that, he should *want* to be a better person.

Guest Appearance from a Real-Life Ex of Mine!

What do men think when they're late? I asked a chronically late exboyfriend of mine. The answer was so simple. "The thought is this," my ex-boyfriend explained. "I'm getting busy. Something just came up. I don't think I'm going to be late, or maybe I'll be a little late, but I don't want to focus on it." Gee, thanks. Fuck off.

A Word from a Grade-A Husband . . .

"My wife is usually the one who's late. So I always bring my BlackBerry and play video games. Anyway, if we're meeting at home, she can be half an hour late. If we're meeting at a bar after work, she can be fifteen minutes late. I've learned never to meet her on a street corner, especially during winter. But when I'm late . . . well, let's just say I have an account at a flower store and I know what her favourite flowers are." (This guy really is too good to be true.)

WISE WORDS FROM HELENA.

She Does My Brazilian Bikini Waxes. She Knows, Hears, and Sees It All!

"I have a strict ten-minute rule. I wait only ten minutes and then I'm gone."
(Don't sugar-coat it for me! Also, remind me never to be late to Helena's.)

CLEVER TACTICS/ADVICE ON RAISING YOUR MAN TO ACHIEVE AT OR ABOVE THE EXPECTED LEVEL

1. If he is always late, don't show up on time.

2. Call him mid-afternoon and remind him of your meeting time. Ask him how his day is looking. You have now reminded him that he should be on time, and if he's not, you're free to speak up.

3. Make him pay if he is late. I do this for everyone who is late. It's a penalty. Eventually, unless he's super rich, it becomes an incentive to be on time.

4. Be a little generous. There is a lot of traffic and construction in this city. People are late. Shit happens. Just don't let him get away with it all the time.

5. Quote Winnie the Pooh (above). He's so cute! Who can argue with Winnie?

6. Remember, a lot of women are late too. I am. Sometimes.

7. Tell him to meet you half an hour earlier than you're really meeting.

CHAPTER TEN

You're Bailing? WTF?

W hen someone cancels on you and you've really been looking forward to seeing that person, it can hurt like a bitch. It stings more in the short term, but it can be better than sitting and stewing about how late someone is. I was dating an investment banker. (I was so traumatized after that relationship, for many reasons, that it took me three months to even walk into a bank.) Time was not his own. He lived in the warped money world, where the stock market and clients always came first, and personal life came last. I realized almost instantly that I would be second in his life, that I wouldn't be his number-one priority. I was okay with this, since I was busy with my job and being a single mother to my daughter. He was not my number-one priority either. But he would always cancel on me. I realized that our relationship wouldn't last after we made plans once and I wondered, "Should I bother to shower and get dressed? There's a 70 percent chance he's going to cancel." You know a relationship is bad when you wonder if you should bother showering because there's a high chance your boyfriend is going to bail.

I knew he was a bailer. I was once at the grocery store buying fresh vegetables for our dinner when he called to say, "I won't be able to make it. Call you later." Of course, things come up. But it's the way you tell me that something has come up that matters. It was definitely over with him when he cancelled on me before a friend's wedding. Cancel on me for dinner, cool. Cancel on being my date for a friend's wedding on a Saturday night? I don't actually mind attending weddings alone. I mind that I had to send my friend an e-mail the night before her wedding saying that I was now coming solo because he had to work on a Saturday night.

"There have been times my husband is so late that it's stupid for him to even show up. I tell him that, and it's like he had never planned to come anyway. I've entertained his clients alone many times," complained one friend. "It's always so uncomfortable and I hate my husband at those times."

But there is something just as bad as cancelling, and that is not making plans in the first place. "He would never cancel on me because he would always be so noncommittal," said another friend. "He'd always say, 'I don't know what time I'll be out of here.' Or, 'I'm not sure if I have to work late.' So he'd never make plans." Another friend is never sure if her husband is going to bail. "His favourite line is 'I'll be there when I'll be there.'" Another girlfriend's boyfriend's line is "I'll meet you there." She hates this. "He'll meet me there? Well, I don't think so. We're dating. We're together. It's rude to tell me to meet you someplace, especially if we're going to a party and I don't know anyone there. It's uncomfortable for me. And he should know better. He should come pick me up, and we should arrive together."

I Just Saved You $200 and Forty-five Minutes of Your Time (Total: $1,800)

Sometimes Freud makes me laugh. Sometimes he's worth $200 just for the chuckles he gives me. Freud, I will say, does come up with some unique ideas. If a man you're dating or married to cancels on you regularly, Freud suggests having a discussion that includes the words "cancellation" and "policy." Just as airlines and hotels have cancellation policies, relationships can have them too. He says that if cancelling is a chronic problem, couples should come up with their own cancellation policy (including getting a doctor's note!). If you cancel, there will be a fine or punishment (unless you have a doctor's note). Even Freud—FREUD—says you can use sex, or rather the withholding of sex, as a penalty. (But depending on how good your sex life is, this can also be a punishment for you, so I'm not sure about that one.) I can, however, think of a list of penalties for a chronically cancelling boyfriend. If you cancel, you have to make the bed for a week. If you cancel, you have to buy me a gift. You cancel? You can put the kids to bed all week. You have to get my car cleaned. I get to pick the movie. You have to make dinner. I get a spa day. This experiment could be so fun! In fact, if we had a cancellation policy, I might look forward to your cancelling on me. I might *beg* you to cancel on me.

CLEVER TACTICS/ADVICE ON RAISING YOUR MAN TO ACHIEVE AT OR ABOVE THE EXPECTED LEVEL

1. Ask up front if he is going to bail. If the answer is maybe, go out and make your own plans. You are not waiting around for him. He'll learn.

2. Follow Freud's advice and tell your man there's a cancellation policy. Have fun with this. You may want him to cancel if you come up with the right punishments.

3. Play the "If the tables were reversed" game. Try it out on him. When he asks to make plans, say, "I may be there. I may not." He'll get it. He won't like it. He'll learn.

CHAPTER ELEVEN

Would You Like Some Cheese with That Whine?

I f you have a chronic complainer as a boyfriend or husband, you should realize that he really is a Grown-up Whiner. I was getting the hunch the man I was in a relationship with was a Grown-up Whiner because he complained more often than my six-year-old. He complained about everything endlessly. He complained about his work nonstop. I listened patiently for the first few months because, hey, who likes work? And anyway, when he complained about his work, it made me forget about mine. I was trying to be a supportive girlfriend, and supportive girlfriends listen to their men's problems. Right? Even after I realized that nothing I said or did made this guy stop complaining, however, I still listened. But I'd be on my laptop searching other cities across the world and perusing their weather forecasts. As he ranted, I'd be thinking, "Wow, it's thirty-one and sunny in Barbados!" And, "Oh, it's raining in Paris."

One night, I wanted to test my theory. Was he really a Grown-up Whiner, or was I being too harsh? I smiled calmly each time a complaint came out of his mouth. Now, I suppose you could say that complaining is a form of communication, or making conversation. And if so, the conversation went like this:

HIM: Why is there such a long lineup for this movie?

ME: Because it just came out.

HIM: Why do people always want to see a movie on opening weekend?

ME: Because it's fun and something to do.

HIM: These tickets are so expensive. Why are movie tickets so expensive?

ME: Because movie tickets have been expensive for the *last fifteen years*.
Do you want popcorn?

HIM: Great, another line.

ME: Well, we *are* at the movie theatre.

HIM: When did popcorn become so expensive?

ME: FIFTEEN YEARS AGO!

Once I understood that I was dating a nonstop whiner, I suddenly became less attracted to him. This was not a good thing. This was a very bad thing. Every time a complaint came out of his mouth–"Why are there so many commercials?" or "Why do tall people always end up sitting in front of me?"–I became less and less attracted. Suddenly, he was no longer hot. I couldn't stop myself from seeing him as a six-year-old boy who said things like "Mommy, why is the lineup so long?" And, "Why can't I have that toy?" Nothing makes you lose interest in a man faster. You realize that he's really just a kid in an adult body, and that he doesn't have the good qualities kids have–like an imagination. In fact, he has the qualities that make you ask, "Why have another child?"

Although I do it with my daughter, I couldn't bring myself to say to him, "Stop whining. I heard you the first time. We're here. Enjoy it, goddamnit." But I felt like saying it. I shoved my mouth full of popcorn instead.

Another time I was with a guy and we went to a fancy hotel bar. I like hotel bars. I like the vibe. We went up to the bar, and he ordered a drink. Next thing I knew, he was sort of screaming at the bartender, "What? Fifteen dollars for a glass of wine? That's insane! Why is it so much money?" I was mortified because A) if you go to a hotel bar, that's how much a drink costs, and B) why was he complaining to the bartender? It's not like she sets the prices.

I tell one of my married friends, who doesn't yet have children, that she should borrow a child, because she too has a husband who is a

HOW IT GOES WITH MY SIX-YEAR-OLD . . .

"I don't like this apple juice,"
my daughter will complain.

"That's all we have."

"But I don't like it."

"It's that or water," I say.

"But it tastes weird."

"Apple juice or water?"

"Okay, I'll have water," my daughter will say.

Grown-up Whiner. "He'll be like, 'Tell me why I should be happy with my life!'" she says. "He'll say that all the time. He'll constantly complain about his job, his hours, his colleagues." My friend has no idea what to do with all his complaints and whines, except to try to cheer him up and tell him to look at the bright side of things. "He would always tell me I was too positive. But he was always looking at the negatives. I wouldn't even get a hello before he launched into his list of complaints."

 ### GUEST APPEARANCE FROM A REAL-LIFE EX OF MINE!

I asked my Grown-up Whiner of an ex why he was always complaining about everything. "How am I supposed to know that?" he answered. "Actually I've gotten a lot better. I guess I was just trying to displace an unease in myself. But I really do have to stop complaining so much." (Wow! Even though he's not a boyfriend anymore, I'm going to give him a C, which indicates that some progress is being made. Too bad I'm not with him anymore!)

CLEVER TACTICS/ADVICE ON RAISING YOUR MAN TO ACHIEVE AT OR ABOVE THE EXPECTED LEVEL

1. Ask him, "What are you? Six?"

2. Point out the positives of the situation.

3. Remind him that you just like being with him. Hopefully, that will shut him up.

4. Women complain too, so cut him some slack.

5. Ask him if he'd like some cheese. When he asks why, say, "Because you obviously like whine." (Hey, I think it's funny.)

CHAPTER TWELVE

What Cave Did You Grow Up In?

Men are like fine wine. They all start out like grapes and it's our job to stomp on them and keep them in the dark until they mature into something you'd like to have dinner with.

ANONYMOUS

"I used to send my son away from the table if he sucked on a fork or ate with his mouth open," one of my mommy friends tells me. Then she started dating a guy who was a "messy" eater. Her boyfriend always left every restaurant they went to with food stains on his shirt. "It was unbelievable. My son was neater than he was," she says.

In my house, we have a general rule that there is to be no animal behaviour at the table. My daughter and I don't eat like animals, we don't act like animals, we don't make animal sounds. We also have the "ABC" rule, which is that we don't show food that's "Already Been Chewed."

I once thought of a boyfriend's eating habits as a "unique quirk" that I could get over. Each time a plate of food was placed in front of him, he would wrap one of his arms around that plate and shove the food into his mouth at a rapid pace, as if it were the first meal he'd eaten in a week or the last meal he would be served EVER. The way he wrapped his arm around his plate so protectively, hovering over the food and shoving it in his mouth, made me think that had grown up during the Depression . . . in an orphanage . . . surrounded by bullies. In reality, there was always a lot of food around when he was growing up, so I'm not sure how or why he ended up that way.

In fact, I found his "unique quirk" while eating so odd that I used to pick food off his plate just to witness his reaction, which was laugh-out-loud funny. I'd take an olive from his plate, let's say, and listen to him yell, "That's mine!" with an expression of panic and then swat my hand away. Which made me laugh. After a few months, I knew we were in a good space, because he'd barely flinch when I'd pick an olive off his plate. (He went from a D to a B, which indicates consistent achievement at the expected level.)

Even men who do share with their wives, unlike my ex, have a problem with it. "When we were dating, we would always share," says one of my friends of her now husband. "I'd have a third and he'd have two-thirds. I'd think, 'Well, I'm still a little hungry.' As we got more serious, we'd still share, and I'd eat half of the plate and he'd eat half. But then I became pregnant and I was so hungry, but he still wanted to share food. I was so terrified of sharing with him. But he liked sharing. I would honestly feel like crying because I'd be so hungry."

Another friend lives through this unique eating quirk with her husband (which means this trait is not that unique with men after all). "He hates to share. It's so annoying. If we go out for sushi, he'll always have to order his own stuff," she says. "He'll cringe when I pick off his plate. I would also suggest to him what he should order, so I could try it. But if I wasn't paying attention, then he would refuse to tell me what he ordered. It was just weird."

For my friend Shelly, who was one of the last of my friends to get married, a man who ate with his mouth open (an ABC-er) was a deal-breaker. Now, you could say that like many women, she had unrealistic expectations for men. People would tell her all the time that she couldn't refuse to date a guy because he ate weird. But the thing is, she waited it out, sticking with her deal-breakers, and she found the perfect man for herself. Aside from one thing—he ate with his mouth open. How is it possible that she ended up with a man who ate with his mouth open? "We didn't eat together on our first date. We just went for a walk and had coffee. We walked and talked for hours, but there was no food involved. So after the first date, I was totally into him," she explains. They went on a second date, which involved dinner, and that's when she realized that he ate with his mouth open. "But by then, I was already so into him." It took her a long time to finally say something about his ABC problem. About six months into their relationship, they went on their first vacation together, to Mexico. At lunch one day, she announced, "I can't eat with you when you chew with your mouth open and talk with food in your mouth. If you don't stop, I'm moving tables." In fact, she went one step further and told him that she couldn't keep dating him if he continued to eat like that.

Now, three happily married years and one child later, that fight in Mexico remains the biggest fight they've ever had. And to this day, she says, her husband doesn't get "what's so wrong" with eating with his mouth open. "He literally still doesn't understand it. But when he's with me, he'll chew with his mouth shut. He does it for me." (Her husband gets an A for effort, at least with her.)

Another friend has tried to explain to her boyfriend, who also eats with his mouth open, that as a big-shot lawyer who travels with big-shot politicians and other clients, he really must try eating with his mouth shut. "I can't imagine him eating out with all these high-powered people the way he eats in front of me," she says. "But who knows? Maybe men don't notice. Or, God forbid, they all eat like that. I try not to think about it."

Other men (not any of mine, thank God) also seem to have a problem when it comes to making *noise* while eating. (Actually, they have a problem when it comes to eating quietly.) Another married friend of mine is constantly nagging her husband not to eat so loudly. "I can hear him in another room, smacking away on food," she explains. "I will scream at him, 'I can hear you,' if he's eating while watching television and I'm in the kitchen. He'll yell back, 'What do you care? We're not even in the same room!'"

Another friend also hates her husband's eating habits. What drives her insane is *what* he eats. "He sits there in front of the television with a huge bottle of Dr. Pepper and gumballs. He'll take two sucks on a gumball, take it out, and put another one in. It's so disgusting. I can't even look at a bottle of Dr. Pepper without getting the shivers. And what grown man, except for my husband, eats fucking gumballs?" she asks.

Another women despises that her husband eats right before bed. "It's a horrible habit," she says. Yet another friend says that her husband eats like a "caveman." "He'll stab his food. He slurps his soup. I can't stand it. It's disgusting." Her husband will just say, "What are you talking about? I'm eating normally." Also, she continues, "He'll blow his nose with his napkin and then wipe the table with it. Need I say more?"

A Word from a Grade-A Husband . . .

"Good manners is about slowing down. That's what I've learned. I used to inhale my food, just because I'm a man and when I'm hungry I just want to get the food down as quickly as possible. But when you slow down, you are less likely to be messy, eat with noises, and be disgusting to watch. I don't want my wife to have to wear a blindfold or avert her eyes when we're eating together. So I just slow down now. And actually, I feel a hell of a lot better after a meal when I eat slower."

CLEVER TACTICS/ADVICE ON RAISING YOUR MAN TO ACHIEVE AT OR ABOVE THE EXPECTED LEVEL

1. Threaten to leave the table. Hey, it worked for my friend.
2. Explain that it's good manners and good practice to eat with your mouth closed. Tell him he'll come across better when he eats with VIPs and clients.
3. Cutely explain that his food looks better. If he loves you, he'll share.
4. Ask him why he's "hurting" the food, and what the food has done to him.
5. Tell him you're going to move tables.

CHAPTER THIRTEEN

Being a Plus One.
When Good Dates Go Bad

Men want the same thing from their underwear that they want from
women—a little bit of support and a little bit of freedom.
JERRY SEINFELD

Men can be evil. Really, really evil. I had a male friend who
once told me he "test-drives" potential girlfriends by purposely taking them to an event where they don't know
anyone. He takes them to a party, let's say, and pretty much
ditches them immediately upon entering the room. Then he watches them
from the bar or other side of the room. If he sees that the woman can
handle being on her own at a party where she doesn't know anyone but
him, and can speak to just about anyone, he'll think highly of her and be
impressed. But if his date clings to him the entire night, searching him out
as he tries to sneak away, he'll most likely never ask her out again.

Yes, it's a pretty cruel way of seeing what kind of person the girl is. (In fact,
it's really cruel.) But no one (including me) wants to be someone's babysit-
ter at a party. However, if you invite me to a party, and it's your crowd or
your work thing, it's your *job* to make me feel comfortable. It is your *duty* to
ask me if I'd like a drink when we walk in. It is your *responsibility* to introduce me to people I don't know. I don't need to be babysat, but I need to
feel that you want me there at your side. And if I do feel that you want me
at your side, I then need to feel that you're truly proud of me on top of that.

Recently I attended a wedding as a Plus One. My date was good. He
introduced me to people, came to the bar with me, danced with me, and

acted very proud to have me there. (He gets an A for achievement at an exceptionally high level.) But that night, I ran into an old high school acquaintance, who, it turns out, was also someone's Plus One. Her "date" was her boyfriend of TWO years. As soon as I saw her face, I knew something was wrong. I could tell that she was furious. She said hi and launched into a rant. "My boyfriend is totally ignoring me," she stormed. I suggested she have a drink, because clearly she needed one (or three) and pronto. "I can't! He made me drive him here so *he* could drink," she cried. For ten minutes (which seemed like an hour), I listened to her say things like "Let's just see if he notices I'm not having a good time." And, "Let's just see if he comes to find me before dinner."

Her boyfriend was treating her abominably, but I wondered how she could be with a man who treated her that way. (Maybe someone out there does have lower expectations than me!)

One of my friends says that whenever she goes to a party with her boyfriend, he acts like a completely different person. "It would be like we weren't even a couple. He'd stay at one side of the room, and I'd do my own thing. It would always make me so angry," she complains.

Now, a BIG part of going to a party or event with a man is the introductions. Introductions are a huge part of going out together. I've been standing beside boyfriends, at events they have invited me to, when others walk up to us. I don't know these people, but my boyfriend clearly does. I stand there, smiling awkwardly at the other couple while they smile awkwardly at me, and all the while my boyfriend just yammers away.

A lot of women are faced with not being introduced by their men. Not only does it make us feel unwelcome, but it's rude! It makes us feel like you're embarrassed about having us at your side. It makes us feel INVISIBLE. Mostly, I've learned, the problem stems from the fact that men don't seem to remember names. How many of us have heard, "I couldn't remember their names or else I would have introduced you"? Still, we doubt, don't we? "Listen, my husband always does that to me," says one of my friends.

"I'll just be standing there and I'm like, 'Hello, introduce your wife!' But I'll admit, I'm bad at it too. I just won't stick my hand out and introduce myself, but I should. I need to be better at that."

Another woman says, "My husband always tells me, 'If I don't introduce you, it's because I forgot their name. So you introduce yourself, and then they'll say their name.'" (I do the same thing. I warn boyfriends that if I don't introduce them, it's because I don't remember the names of the people I'm speaking to.) Also, we women don't like to babysit our men during parties either. One of my friends stopped bringing her boyfriend to work events. "He never really wanted to come, and also I would have to babysit him," she explained. "I couldn't have any fun because I'd be so worried that he wasn't having fun. I'd see him standing alone and I'd feel obligated to make sure he was okay. Eventually, he'd suggest that he leave before me, and I'd say, 'That's a good idea.'"

Parties are fraught with other issues as well. There are the men who go AWOL during parties. Sometimes you're wondering if they've left, because they couldn't possibly be in the washroom that long and the room isn't *that* big. This happened to me at my prom, and I'm still traumatized. My boyfriend—my first real boyfriend—decided to leave to go to a bar with some guys . . . in the middle of *prom*. Fifteen years later, I still feel as if men like to pull this disappearing act. "My husband is always so happy to see his friends that he forgets he brought me, his wife!" one woman tells me. "I'll be looking for him and asking people if they've seen him, and everyone thinks I'm an idiot for losing him, probably wondering if we're getting along. Meanwhile, he's just stepped outside for a couple of cigarettes with some people. I don't smoke. But I think, at the very least, he could have the courtesy to tell me he's leaving me for thirty minutes. Or ask me to join him outside."

GUEST APPEARANCE FROM A
REAL-LIFE EX OF MINE!

"Men! God bless them," one of my exes says when I ask him about male behaviours at events or parties. "Men need and want to be in a couple, but they are in a constant rebellion mode. They don't want to be Mr. Domestic. They go to a party and they want to forget they are in a relationship or married. They think, 'Great! If I want to talk to my wife, I can. But I don't have to.' And when a woman comes up to a man at a party, and we are in the middle of a great conversation with even another guy, all guys know that, chances are, your wife is going to join you. And she's not joining to join in the conversation. She's joining to tamp the conversation down. When the wife or girlfriend comes over, what she's saying by coming up is 'Include me.' Women feel like their guys have a time limit. Women are checking in. But men don't check in on men. God, as I get older I realize my behaviour is outrageous! But what I'm saying is the truth." (*At least* he realizes his behaviour is outrageous. That's something.)

A WORD FROM A GRADE-A HUSBAND . . .

"When I was dating, that was always an issue. Girls were always saying to me, if I took them to a party or wedding as a date, 'I didn't feel like we were together.' Or they'd say, 'I felt like you were embarrassed of me.' And in almost all of the cases, that was *not* the case. But now, I go out of my way to kiss my wife in public. Also, if we have a lot of friends over for a barbecue or something, I'll always give her a foot massage. Giving the woman in your life a foot massage in public is a super-demonstrative sign that you're with her."

CLEVER TACTICS/ADVICE ON RAISING YOUR MAN TO ACHIEVE AT OR ABOVE THE EXPECTED LEVEL

1. Tell him you're a little nervous before the party/event and it would be nice if he made sure you were okay.

2. Always have a drink first. It makes things easier. But don't overdo it.

3. Don't be shy! Introduce yourself! You'll feel good that you're the type of woman who is brave enough to do so.

4. Don't hang on to your guy. Act confident!

5. If he is rude, leave. You'll be in a bad mood, but being in a bad mood at home is better than being in a bad mood at a party.

CHAPTER FOURTEEN

The PDA.
Don't You Want to Let the World Know I'm Yours?

———————

Unlike the Grade-A Husband, most men are so bad with the PDA, the public display of affection. "My husband will never put his arm around me, never holds my hand," one of my friends says. I once was in a relationship with a guy who wouldn't even let me hold his hand while he was driving. And we were in a car! He would look at me like "What are you doing?" One male friend tells me that most guys don't like holding hands because "it feels goofy. It feels like we're seven years old again and with Mom."

I like the public display of affection. It makes me feel nice to see couples holding hands or walking with their arms around each other. It gives me hope. As long as I don't see tongue, or anything that should be taken to a hotel room, I think PDA is cute. I enjoy seeing it. And when my daughter hugs me or kisses me or says "I love you" in public, there's not a dry eye on the street. Honestly, she'll kiss me on the cheek and hands will flutter to hearts.

 I JUST SAVED YOU $200 AND FORTY-FIVE MINUTES OF YOUR TIME (TOTAL: $2,000)

"It has to do with intimacy issues. One of the first questions I ask patients is if they saw their parents show affection to each other. Because that's telling," says Freud. But he agrees with me that seeing other people acting romantic in public makes us feel good. And gives us hope!

Guest Appearance from a Real-Life Ex of Mine!

When I called to ask one of my exes why he was so bad at the public display of affection, his immediate response was "I can't take this!" But then, because he still does like me, he tried to answer to the best of his ability. "It's such a self-conscious thing to wrap your arms around someone. It's sissy. Listen, did you really want to walk into a dinner party with me holding my hand?" ("Yes!" I told him.) "Well, I showed you my affection privately. Anyway, men are warriors. They can't have a shackle around them." (To which I responded, "Huh?") Then he added, "If you have a trophy wife, then the guy is proud to hold her hand or wrap his arms around her. Because it not only shows men that my gal is really hot, but also shows women that 'Hey, I got her. So I can get you too.'" (To which I responded, "So you didn't feel like I was good-looking enough to be a 'trophy'?" Then he got all flustered, and we got into a little bickering match, which reminded me of why we're not together.)

A Word from a Grade-A Husband . . .

"Ah, parties. I never leave my wife out of any conversation. I never stay away from her for any long period of time. I give her space if she's enjoying a conversation, but I certainly don't peel off as soon as we get there. In fact, I sometimes feel bad for her at parties. I can see the look on her face when I'm telling a story that she's already heard five times. I can see her just staring blankly or thinking, 'That didn't *really* happen the way you're telling it.' But she'll put up with me."

CLEVER TACTICS/ADVICE ON RAISING YOUR MAN TO ACHIEVE AT OR ABOVE THE EXPECTED LEVEL

1. Point out how sweet another couple is.

2. Make the move. Grab his hand.

3. Say, "I feel like a hug!" What guy is going to deny you that small pleasure?

4. Tell him that it's foreplay, and that when you get home, they'll be more where that came from. Tell him that the PDA will turn into something R-rated.

5. Maybe you don't like PDA either. So do you really care?

6. Remind yourself that maybe he is affectionate when you are alone.

CHAPTER FIFTEEN

You're Not Really Going to Wear That, Are You?

⸺⸻⸺

After getting out of the relationship with the investment banker, I was sick of the suits. Meaning, I was sick of dating suits. I was over suits. (Except that I'm *not* really over suits. I love a man in a nice suit.) I started dating a self-employed web designer who worked out of his home. I thought it was brilliant! He didn't own one suit. I loved how he wore ripped T-shirts. There was absolutely nothing in his closet (or on his bedroom floor) that needed dry cleaning. It was a breath of fresh air. Until, that is, his wardrobe, or lack of one, started to annoy me. I wondered how he could go out in public with his fly undone and holes in his T-shirt. And then I fell into the trap that many, many, many women have fallen into before me, are falling into as we speak, and probably will fall into in the future. I was out shopping for myself at a sample sale when I saw a men's sweater. It was nice. "My new guy would look good in this sweater," I found myself thinking. I looked at the price tag. A steal for this designer sweater! And how nice was it that I was looking at clothes for him while shopping for myself? I couldn't wait to see his face light up when he saw that I had bought him a new sweater. It was that easy to fall into it. Soon, whenever I went shopping for myself, I always ended up in the men's section, just to look. That's how men get us. They know that if they continue to wear their ripped T-shirts, then we'll have to go buy them clothes if we want to be seen in public with them! Sneaky men. Do they plan this? Do they know that we're going to get sick of seeing them looking homeless, sick of harassing them about their stained shirts, and will just end up buying them clothes?

Maybe. It happened to a girlfriend of mine. "I'd have no choice but to buy him clothes. He was so cheap and he didn't have any sense of style. I became his personal shopper," she says. But even men who do buy their own clothes seem to have a problem choosing appropriate attire to wear. "We were going for dinner to a semi-nice place and he comes downstairs wearing those sandals with Velcro, the type you used to wear at overnight camp, and a T-shirt. He's a mess!" my friend says to me when I ask her about her husband and how he dresses. "I just tell him to go change. Or I pick out the clothes for him and tell him what to wear. You know, like actual shoes that cover his toes!"

Another woman complains, "I have to remind him that we're not going golfing. I'm like, 'Come on! We're going to a funeral. You're a grown man. Dress appropriately!'"

Other women have fallen into the trap I did. Like I said, it just happens. "When I first met my husband, he picked me up on our first date in a pair of jeans with ten keys hanging off his belt buckle. He also had an earring and wore this awful silver ring that had this wizard thing on it. It was horrifying," says one woman I know, not bothering to hide her disgusted expression. Now she buys him all his clothes. Yet even that is not enough.

HOW IT GOES WITH MY SIX-YEAR-OLD . . .

"What are you wearing?" I'll say.

"I picked it out myself,"
my daughter will say proudly.

"Yes, I can see that," I'll say.

"Don't I look pretty?" she'll ask.

"You sure do. I love that you're wearing a yellow tank top over a pink long-sleeve shirt, and that your pants are purple. And that ballet tutu over it? Genius! And the fact that you're wearing two different socks? Gorgeous!"

(She's six. She's ALLOWED to get away with it. People think it's cute. But not so much with men!)

"I just bought him a pair of yoga pants that need to be shortened. He told me, 'But I'll never make it to get it done!' I'm like, 'Yes, you will make it there! You haven't bought a piece of clothes for yourself in eight years! The least you can do is get one pair of pants shortened."

Many men, it turns out, have never shopped for themselves. EVER! One man I know, at forty-two, has never bought one item of clothing for himself. Ever. (Have I said EVER?) His mother bought him clothes until he moved out, with help from his sister. Then his girlfriends bought him clothes. And now his wife does.

Another friend of mine gets into arguments all the time with her husband over his clothes (which, depending on your sensibility, is either a good thing or a bad thing). She came up with a brilliant plan for when her husband wears something she hates. At least it works brilliantly for her. "I can't convince him not to wear something. However, I can mock him enough that he doesn't wear it again," she explains. Her husband's sweater with big yellow stripes? "I just kept making fun of him all day, calling him the bumblebee, asking him if he was a bumblebee, stuff like that. He also had this awful white dress shirt that made him look like a pirate. I kept making fun of that shirt." She never saw the yellow sweater or the white dress shirt again. "Like I said, I can't make him not wear something, but if I mock him enough, he won't wear it again."

The following argument actually happened between a friend and her boyfriend:

HER: You don't look straight in that outfit.
HIM: So? Gay men dress really well.
HER: Not *all* gay men dress really well.

Another married friend moaned about her husband's sloppy long-sleeve shirt, which was way too tight and had stains. "He didn't give a shit about his appearance. I'm like, 'You can see your man boobs!' I would ask him to put on something else that was a little more flattering, and his answer would always be 'What do you care?' I'd say, 'Because I want you to look CLEAN!'"

I once dated a guy who had the most horrific jeans. He refused to throw them out, however. So one day, I threw them out. I not only threw them out, but threw them over the balcony of the condo where he lived. Ha! (Yeah, I'm not always the nicest person. But it worked. The jeans were GONE FOREVER!)

Other men go as far as complaining about what we wear when they dress like shit. "My husband will tell me, 'You cannot wear that out. It's tattered.' The next day, he'll be wearing clothes with paint stains and rips under the arm," one woman tells me.

GUEST APPEARANCE FROM A
REAL-LIFE EX OF MINE!

This ex, while not always a bad boyfriend, is definitely cynical when it comes to relationships. And lazy too. "If you care that much about how I dress, then why don't you put out my wardrobe for me and I'll put it on?" he complains. "But I think women secretly want their men to look slightly slobby. They say they want you to look good, so they'll spend time buying you nice clothes, and then they see you in them at a party and they think to themselves, 'I just clothed him and made him look hot. Now other girls are looking at him.' So then they get jealous. So, yes, secretly I do think women want us to not look our best. With guys, we want our women to look hot!" (This ex can get away with saying this, and believing this, because he really is model handsome. Personally, I think it's bullshit that women secretly want their guys to look like shit.)

WISE WORDS FROM HELENA.
She Does My Brazilian Bikini Waxes. She Knows, Hears, and Sees It All!
"Do most of my clients like how their husbands or boyfriends dress?
Do you mean do they like what they buy them to wear? They don't seem to
mind buying their partners clothes. Hey, what woman doesn't like shopping?
Don't you love shopping?" (*Yeah, yeah. I do. I really do.*)

CLEVER TACTICS/ADVICE ON RAISING YOUR MAN TO ACHIEVE AT OR ABOVE THE EXPECTED LEVEL

1. Mock him (gently) about what he is wearing. Hey, it worked for my friend!

2. Don't start buying him clothes. It's a trap.

3. Don't attack him. Say instead, "I saw something you may like. You should check it out."

4. Suggest a good salesperson you know.

5. If you buy him something, buy yourself something as well. You deserve it!

6. Hide the items you hate. Just do it. Or throw them off the balcony.

CHAPTER SIXTEEN

Shopping with Men. Like Swimming with Sharks, but Worse

The finest clothing made is a person's skin, but,
of course, society demands something more than this.
MARK TWAIN *(By "society" he must be talking about women. Hee hee.)*

There will come a time, usually early on in a relationship, when you'll ask your guy to come shopping with you. He will do it, because he wants to please you. Flash forward a few months or a few years, and he will not like doing it. He may come with you, but while you try on clothes, he'll plop himself down on the "man chair" and talk on the phone or text his friends. But, my God, I realized only recently that there also comes a time when your man will want *you* to come shopping with him. Let's just say that unless you are the most patient shopper and unconditionally love your man, this will not be a fun moment in your life. At least it wasn't for me. I always thought that men didn't like shopping. But the man who asked me to go shopping with him was more insecure and indecisive when it came to picking clothes than most females I know.

When I come out of a changeroom and the guy nods in approval or says, "That looks great," I'll usually buy whatever I'm trying on, because it got the boyfriend stamp of approval. But when I shopped with one of my boyfriends, I tried to be helpful. "Try these and these and these," I said, handing him three pairs of shoes. Now, I may not be Anna Wintour, but I do know shoes. I know what I'd like to see on my boyfriend's feet, and what I defi-nitely *don't* want to see on my boyfriend's feet. "Really? These?" he kept asking. "I love them," I told him. "But you're the one who has to wear them." "I guess I like them," he said. "They're great," I told him, for maybe the fortieth time. But it wasn't me who convinced him that the shoes were fabu-lous. It was the three female sales clerks. So why wasn't it good enough that I said they were great? Why did it take three female strangers to convince him that the shoes were good? Who was he dating? The sales gals or me? I'd almost rather have seen him with holes in his shoes than be bothered going shopping with him again.

One of my friends gets this. Her guy hates shopping but drags her along. It infuriates her. Why? "Because he'll literally go up to the sales girl and say, 'Where are the cheapest racks of clothes?'" And this guy has money! He just doesn't want to spend his money on clothes.

Guest Appearance from a Real-Life Ex of Mine!

I called an ex who liked to wear T-shirts. That's fine. I like a guy in T-shirts. Except that every one of his T-shirts had holes under the armpits. Why do guys get holes under their armpits? Why do guys spend so much time in the washroom? It's a mystery. "You know, women dress up not for men but for other women," he explained. "Women know if you're wearing Manolo what-are-they-called. You know, most men want their chicks in blue jeans and a T-shirt, not all dolled up. Do men dress up for other men? No."

CLEVER TACTICS/ADVICE ON RAISING YOUR MAN TO ACHIEVE AT OR ABOVE THE EXPECTED LEVEL

1. Tell him he looks great in something when he comes out of the changeroom. Tell him he looks *so* good you want to rip his clothes off.

2. Buy him a gift certificate for a personal shopper.

3. Remind yourself that you really do like shopping, so it's no big deal if you have to help him pick out clothes.

4. Remind him he's not dating the salesgirl. He's dating you!

5. If you go shopping with him, he has to go shopping with you. Tell him that, and maybe he won't ask you to come along.

CHAPTER SEVENTEEN

Baggage (and Not the Louis Vuitton Kind). I'm Talking About the Ex. Why Won't She Go Away?

A fter dating a few men who definitely needed to be "raised," I realized that I was coming up with some of my own bottom lines. It's like learning a new language. One day, you realize that you can speak it and understand it! I realized what I wanted (and needed) in a boyfriend. And I realized what I didn't want in a boyfriend. I didn't want a boyfriend who acted like he was still married to his ex.

Now, at my age (and the age of anyone I would date), we all have baggage. Any man over the age of thirty will have baggage. If you're lucky, he'll just have an ex-girlfriend or two. But he may even have ex-wives. He may even have EX-WIVES and CHILDREN.

There is nothing worse than an ex-girlfriend or ex-wife who will not go away. Make that, there is nothing worse than an ex-girlfriend or ex-wife who will not go away because your boyfriend does not really want her to go away. (Or at least he won't tell her, in better words, to back the FUCK off.)

I know what I speak of. One of my serious relationships after my split was with a man who had been married for a decade. Though he and his ex had divorced, I often asked myself (and a whole bunch of girlfriends) if his ex-wife *realized* that she was an *ex*-wife. That's because, aside from not being sexually intimate with him, she still did very wifely things for him. In fact, she was nicer to him than I was. I once walked into his apartment (which his ex-wife found for him) to see it newly decorated (his ex-wife found the decorator), with a vase of fresh flowers on his kitchen table (his ex-wife had a key and bought the flowers for him).

(Sorry, had to take a break and walk around the block. Still fuming. I'm back now.)

If I date you and you have children with your ex, I get that you need to stay in touch. But this guy didn't have kids with his ex. His ex-wife knew that he was dating me, because he told her he was.

Of course I was angry that she was still so much a part of his life. We got into many fights about her. In fact, I remember yelling, "Next to your mother, I should be the number-one priority in your life." (Okay, not one of my proudest moments. Again, I'm not perfect. The thing was, I really felt that, next to his mother, I should be his number-one priority.)

"Don't you think it's nice that they can still have an amicable relationship?" Freud asked me, after I went on a rampage about my boyfriend's ex-wife during one appointment. "Don't you think it's better than them hating each other?"

"But don't you think it's disrespectful to me?" I shot back. "Shouldn't *I* be the one helping him find a place to live? Shouldn't *I* be the one to be asked for decorating tips? Shouldn't he be coming to *me*?"

Freud kind of got my point. Kind of. He told me to talk to him about it. So I did. My boyfriend seemed to get it too, because he stopped seeing her. Kidding! Actually, he didn't stop seeing her. He just lied to me when he did see her, and then I would find out, and it wouldn't be good. (He had very good qualities. He was very supportive. He was great in bed and a good cook! And he didn't get mad when something last minute came up with my daughter and I'd have to cancel on him.)

But then, his ex asked him to drive her to the airport and told him that if he did, he could have her car for the week. I lost it. Because, hey, driving someone to the airport is a very intimate thing to do, isn't it? I mean, my friends don't even ask me to do that!

So I moaned about this to Freud during our next appointment. "You're right. Boundaries need to be made," he said. (Duh! That's what I was *trying* to tell him the last time. Why was I paying $200 again?)

One of my best friends married a divorced man with three children. I moaned to her about my boyfriend's ex-wife. Surely, she'd understand. "I totally get it," she said. "I would go to soccer games with my husband when we first got engaged, to watch their son play, and he and his ex would start talking about old times and laughing over inside jokes only they understood. I put an end to that immediately by explaining that it made me feel left out and hurt my feelings."

But then she told me that I had to stop blaming the ex-wife. "What do you mean I can't blame her? She's treating him like they're still married. If I can't blame her, whom can I blame? I need to blame someone!" I screamed.

"Him!" she announced. "Your boyfriend! Blame him! He's enabling her! Why would he ask her to stop doing all these nice things for him?" She was right! Why *would* he ask her to stop doing all these nice things for him? It was an aha moment.

So I sat down with my boyfriend and explained, for better or worse, that it was her or me. He would have to decide. He told me, point blank, that he wanted to always be friends with her, but that he understood my position. Then he started to come to me with things he used to rely on his ex for. I felt hopeful. Until I realized that good old saying "Be careful what you wish for" was actually true!

To give him credit, my boyfriend did live up to his word. He came to me with the problems and issues he used to rely on his wife to handle. I should have been happy, right? But I was getting phone calls *all* the fucking time with his problems, which included "Should I get blinds for my bedroom?" Or, "What should I do today?" And, "I have a sore throat. Do you think I should go to the doctor?"

As you can see, this man was so NOT RAISED that he couldn't even make a decision on his own. No longer did I feel like his girlfriend. I completely felt like his mother. I wanted to say to him, "Can you please bring your ex-wife back into the picture. Pretty please?"

When we broke up, I felt like I had dodged a bullet. "Ex-wife," I thought, "you can have him!"

When it comes to baggage, everyone has some. But it's the way you carry it that matters. Men know that women have issues with exes. For example, one of my friends' husbands insisted to her that one of his female friends had only ever been a friend. "Seven years later, we got drunk and he admitted that they had made out a few times. Which means many times. It took him SEVEN years to admit that to me, even though I knew it all along in my gut."

 I JUST SAVED YOU $200 AND FORTY-FIVE
MINUTES OF YOUR TIME (TOTAL: $2,200)

Freud does say it's better that exes remain friendly; however, boundaries need to be made. "There's a difference between meeting an ex for lunch and having dinner with them on a Friday night. There's a difference between meeting for a quick drink after work and going to a concert with them," he says.

WISE WORDS FROM HELENA.
She Does My Brazilian Bikini Waxes. She Knows, Hears, and Sees It All!
"Actually, my husband's ex is very nice. She lives in Paris now, and she just called the other week to talk to me. She's actually a very lovely person. We had a very pleasant conversation. And I don't feel threatened because he's with me." (God, Helena, along with being witty, is sometimes so damn reasonable and generous. Which is why I love her.)

CLEVER TACTICS/ADVICE ON RAISING YOUR MAN
TO ACHIEVE AT OR ABOVE THE EXPECTED LEVEL

1. Say, "I don't have a problem with you seeing your ex for a coffee. But I'm going to get angry if you go out to dinner and come home at 2 a.m."

2. Remind yourself that he's yours. Don't act threatened. You're the bomb, and he's lucky to be with you.

3. Remind yourself that there is a reason she's the *ex.*

4. Try never to say anything bad about the ex. Be classy.

CHAPTER EIGHTEEN

Being Friends with the Opposite Sex. Just Friends?

HARRY: Because no man can be friends with a woman that he finds
    attractive. He always wants to have sex with her.

SALLY: So you're saying that a man can be friends with a woman he
    finds unattractive?

HARRY: No. You pretty much want to nail 'em too.

SALLY: What if *they* don't want to have sex with you?

HARRY: Doesn't matter, because the sex thing is already out there, so the
    friendship is ultimately doomed and that is the end of the story.

SALLY: Well, I guess we're not going to be friends, then.

HARRY: I guess not.

SALLY: That's too bad. You were the only person I knew in New York.

    (FROM THE MOVIE *When Harry Met Sally,* 1989)

I think it's important to have friends of the opposite sex. One of my good male friends will come with me to see any movie I want. He's my movie friend. Another male friend has great taste when it comes to clothes, and great advice when it comes to what men are thinking, so he gives me advice about my boyfriends and comes with me clothes shopping. But many of my married friends don't have good guy friends. One of my married friends says that her husband wouldn't like it. It's that simple. She loves her husband, doesn't want him to be jealous, and so doesn't go out with other men.

In a moment I'm not too proud of, I told one of my boyfriends that he could meet up with an ex-girlfriend for coffee or lunch and speak on the phone with her occasionally, but he couldn't have anything to do with her after six o'clock. The reasoning behind this was that there should be boundaries, like Freud told me. You may be wondering where I came up with this "no meeting after six o'clock" rule. Well, I got it from another woman, of course! This woman was uncomfortable with her professor-husband hanging out after work at bars with other colleagues (and, gulp, female students).

"You can't have a problem with them having friends of the opposite sex, even if you don't like it," sighs one of my girlfriends. "Then they'll just end up lying." She's right.

I Just Saved You $200 and Forty-five Minutes of Your Time (Total: $2,400)

When I tell Freud about the "no meeting after six o'clock rule," he tells me that's ridiculous. "If a guy is going to cheat, and that's what she's worried about, it can happen at any time."

Guest Appearance from a Real-Life Ex of Mine!

"If a woman doesn't have any guy friends, I think that means she doesn't understand men or fundamentally doesn't like men. If a woman doesn't have any guy friends that means that she is excluding 50 percent of the population for no other reason than their sex. Or maybe no guys like you. That can tell you a lot," he says. (Though it is an interesting concept, do you buy this?)

CHAPTER NINETEEN

Flirting. Yes, She's Cute, but She Doesn't Have Anything in Her Teeth, So Stop Staring!

In any bar, in any city, one can find a hundred beautiful girls. But they don't have your charm, your brain, your sense of humour! (That's what I tell myself.) I'm pretty serious about my boyfriends not overly flirting in front of me. But I assume that they act flirty when I'm not around, and I sometimes flirt when they're not around. In fact, I sometimes flirt when they *are* around to make them feel a tinge of jealousy. So I can only assume that if they do flirt in front of me, they are expecting the same response. But noticing a gorgeous girl is okay. I notice gorgeous men. I'm not dead. I'm human. And our men are human too. One woman I know got really pissed off at her boyfriend, and rightfully so, when they attended a wedding. He had forgotten to compliment her, but when he met the bride's sister, he kept going on and on about how gorgeous she was—to his girlfriend! "I couldn't believe it," she says. "It was so lame and so hurtful. He didn't even realize he was doing it. Say it once, fine. But to say it over and over again?" Let's just say that night didn't turn out so well. What can I say about her boyfriend? He's an idiot. (Or at least he was in that moment.)

Flirting can be harmless. People who are secure in their relationships, I find, tend to be more flirtatious. Why? Because it doesn't matter. There's no fear of rejection. One of my male friends says that in every single one of his relationships, there were always three issues: 1) the woman never felt like a priority, 2) he was too flirtatious, and 3) he could never commit.

I Just Saved You $200 and Forty-five Minutes of Your Time (Total: $2,600)

Freud says that his wife once told him, "The day you stop looking at other women, that's the day I'll start to worry." So I asked, "Why? Because she'll realize you're gay?" No, he answered, because it's "human nature" to look. I argue that it's okay to look, but it's not okay for a man to go on and on and on about how gorgeous someone is. "It's okay to look within boundaries. One glance is okay. A second glance is not okay. If you're in a happy, stable relationship, you're not going to care if your partner is checking someone else out." He says that if a guy looks once, he's only checking a woman out. Twice, there's an attraction. If he continues to stare, it's inappropriate.

WISE WORDS FROM HELENA.
She Does My Brazilian Bikini Waxes. She Knows, Hears, and Sees It All!
"I hope he looks at good-looking women!
I tell him he can check out the menu,
but he has to come home for dinner. I tell him he can look
at the menu, but he can't sample the goods."

CLEVER TACTICS/ADVICE ON RAISING YOUR MAN TO ACHIEVE AT OR ABOVE THE EXPECTED LEVEL

1. Tell him what Helena says. He can check out the menu, but he has to come home for dinner.

2. Remind yourself that it's NORMAL to check out good-looking people.

3. Don't overreact.

4. You're hot stuff. He may look, but remember, he's with you!

5. Suggest that you all get together. I'm never really interested in meeting my boyfriends' exes or female friends, but at least it could be a funny experience.

CHAPTER TWENTY

The Washroom. Seriously, What Are You Doing in There?

———

"I really think the key to a happy marriage is two washrooms," says my friend from university. When she first started dating her husband, she couldn't figure out why his garbage can was right in front of his toilet. "I just thought his cleaning lady had washed the floors and had left it in the wrong place," she says. But week after week, every time she used his washroom, she'd find the garbage can right back in front of the toilet. It was only after they bought a house together—with more than one washroom—that she learned the garbage can is always in front of his toilet because he brings his laptop to the washroom to work and e-mail while he . . . you know. "Honestly," she repeats, "the key to a happy marriage is two washrooms." (I also think the key to a happy relationship is a housekeeper.)

If her husband is in his washroom for a long time, she'll actually e-mail him, instead of standing outside and pounding on the door. "I'm ready to go. Is this going to be a long one?" she'll write. So I guess there's a silver lining to the man who works in the washroom on his computer. He gets her e-mails.

My daughter, at age six, knows that she is only to use the girl washrooms at her school, even though they are individual washrooms. She said to me, "Why do boys pee on the floor and seat?" Good question. One I'd love to answer. So I do. "Boys are disgusting," I told her. It's one of the best life lessons I can give her. She should know this sooner than later.

Men *are* a little disgusting. But what woman doesn't remember a first sleepover and having to do number two and freaking out that the guy will smell what we've just done and then realize that we're not just pretty females who always smell good?

"Yes, we're vain," says one of my married friends. "My husband, every morning, he needs his time to poo. But that's not what annoys me. We get two subscriptions to newspapers at home, and he takes them both in there with him. Honestly, he spends so long in there, it got to the point where I'd have to shower while he was doing his business or I'd be late." Um, yuck!

After I had my daughter, I became way more comfortable talking about bowel movements. Possibly this is because I was always asking, "Did you take a poo?" Or, "Do you need to take a poo?" Or, "Maybe you should try pooing." Sometimes I still have to help her wipe her own ass, so all hell breaks loose. I dated a guy for a while and I would announce, "Okay, I'm going to go poo." And he'd be like, "No, seriously. Do you have to say that? Why do you have to talk like that?" So boys too don't want to know what we're doing in there.

One of my friends actually makes her husband sit down when he pees. "I don't care if it's weird. I'll go into the washroom and I'll step in something wet, and I'm not sure if it's from the shower or because he missed the toilet. I rather not take the chance," she explains.

Another friend doesn't understand why her husband goes to the washroom four times a day, for thirty minutes. "And he always goes at the worst times, like when the baby wakes up or a piece of furniture is being delivered." I had another boyfriend who liked to say, "I have to go drop the kids off." And he didn't have any kids to drop off. He said this whenever he had to poo. Yup. Well, I laughed. At least the first few times he said this.

 ## Guest Appearance from a Real-Life Ex of Mine!

The ex I called to ask about washroom habits refused to explain what he did in the washroom for so long. However, he did say, "In the two years I've known you, I think you went to the washroom maybe twice when you were with me." Exactly! And guess what? Men don't want to share the washroom with us. I asked one of my male friends about washrooms and relationships, and he said, "A man and a woman should never share a washroom." He spent two weeks with a girlfriend in France, and to his knowledge, she never once took a crap. "Sometimes she would suggest we go to a restaurant or the hotel bar for a drink, and then she'd disappear for fifteen minutes to 'fix her makeup.' I had a lot of respect for that."

CLEVER TACTICS/ADVICE ON RAISING YOUR MAN TO ACHIEVE AT OR ABOVE THE EXPECTED LEVEL

1. Try not to think about it. It's better that way.
2. Try to have two washrooms when you live together.
3. Keep air freshener and matches in the washroom.
4. Grab the newspaper first!
5. Put an alarm clock in the washroom and set it.

CHAPTER TWENTY-ONE

Gas (Not at the Pumps). It's Really NOT Funny

My daughter farts all the time. She's six and thinks it's funny. And she's allowed to think it's funny, because when you're six, it *is* funny. But she'll always excuse herself after. Because I've drummed that into her head. "Hello? Can you say 'Excuse me' or leave the room?" Need I say more? My friend's husband has the worst gas. When they're invited for dinner at someone's house and she's asked if they have any dietary restrictions, she'll answer, "We're *both* lactose-intolerant." She says, "My husband will be like, 'No, we're not,' but I don't want to deal with his gas all night."

A Word from a Grade-A Husband . . .

"I just shut the door and say, 'Baby, don't go in there.' But women have a harder time saying this," he says. Yes, we do. It's embarrassing. It's part of life. But it's still embarrassing for us.

WISE WORDS FROM HELENA. She Does My Brazilian Bikini Waxes. She Knows, Hears, and Sees It All!
"Yes, men fart in front of you. I'm like, 'How dare you?!' I would never! I had one serious ex-boyfriend before I got married who I literally told, 'If you don't put a cork up your ass, I'm going to.' I told him I pass gas, but for some reason, I DON'T DO IT IN FRONT OF OTHER PEOPLE!"

CLEVER TACTICS/ADVICE ON RAISING YOUR MAN TO ACHIEVE AT OR ABOVE THE EXPECTED LEVEL

1. Ask him if he could leave the room. Or at least say "Excuse me."

2. Tell him it turns you off.

3. Laugh about it, if you can.

4. Threaten, like Helena, to put a cork in it.

5. Remember, guys and girls are different. This is one of those situations where it is *very* clear they are different.

6. Tell him it's not funny.

7. Ask him when you last farted in front of him.

CHAPTER TWENTY-TWO

Take the Hint: We Want Our Alone Time

Women need real moments of solitude and self-reflection
to balance out how much of ourselves we give away.
BARBARA DE ANGELIS

I was having a business meeting with a girlfriend who works out of her house. There's a cute coffee place we always meet at, just across the street from her house. I park in her driveway. When we walked out of the coffee shop and she saw her husband's car in the driveway, her face fell. It literally FELL. "Great," she said, "my husband's home." Now, make no mistake: They are loyal to each other. They communicate well. They talk highly of each other and are supportive. After fourteen years of marriage, they are still attracted to each other. "It's just that when he's home, I can't get any work done," my friend mutters. "He putters around and makes a lot of noise."

Another friend, who is a doctor, often comes home exhausted. "I need to have some time to decompress, and my husband just won't let me be. I just want to lie down for fifteen minutes, and he can't stand it. I'm like, 'I leave you alone when you need alone time, so give me the same courtesy.'"

 GUEST APPEARANCE FROM A
REAL-LIFE EX OF MINE!

I'm a person who needs alone time. I need, like, *a lot* of alone time. I like to sit and eat in front of my television by myself, for example. Or at the end of a long day, when I've been talking on the phone all day or taking meetings,

I just want to sit *in silence* and be. I asked an ex, who would get annoyed that I got annoyed when he kept yapping away when I needed alone time and silence, if he understood this now. "You were so not good when you had a long day. But you were good at telling me you wanted to be alone. You told me that all the time. If you tell someone you need alone time . . . well, that's a pretty good hint that you need alone time. You had it good with me. When you looked at me like you wanted to kill me, I knew you needed alone time. When you stopped laughing at my jokes, I knew you needed alone time." (Not to be picky here, but sometimes his jokes weren't all that funny!)

CLEVER TACTICS/ADVICE ON RAISING YOUR MAN TO ACHIEVE AT OR ABOVE THE EXPECTED LEVEL

1. Bring home from your next vacation a "Do Not Disturb" sign from a hotel room. Nothing gets the message across more clearly that You Do Not Want to Be Disturbed than a sign. (Plus you don't have to say anything.) Have a stack of these on hand!

2. Saying something like, "I've been talking all day long to people. I can't wait for silence," then adding, "I'm going to go enjoy some well deserved quiet time upstairs for a while," should get the point across.

3. If you're like me, you're upfront. I simply say I need "Rebecca Time," which means "Get out of my face." Or I say, "I don't feel like talking right now." Sometimes, once I say it, I realize that I actually do want to talk after all.

4. Remember, if you don't live with your boyfriend, you can get a lot of alone time. It's very easy to turn your communication devices to "silent." It feels weird at first, but you will easily get used to it.

Last Call.
No, It's NOT Okay to Bring
Your Drunk-Ass Friends
Home for a Nightcap

———⬧———

"He doesn't understand," moans one of my friends. "He'll be out with the guys and then he'll for some reason invite a couple of them back to our place for a beer. Hello? We have two children. We both have to work tomorrow. It's a weeknight. Of course, I look like a bitch. I barely say hello to them, and of course, they scurry out so quickly. My husband will get so mad at me, because he thinks I embarrassed him in front of his friends. But where are his priorities?"

Another friend explains that she and her husband are so different. "I like to go to bed early because I'm a bitch if I don't get a good night's sleep. And when we first started dating, our place was where everyone would come back to party. But let's face it: I'm older now. I want to sleep. I'm not interested in partying until 2 a.m. But my husband still is. I just tell him to go out. I tell him it's *not* okay to bring his friends back."

Another girlfriend puts up with her husband's weekly poker nights. "It's not too bad, because his friends will come over only once a month. But I do dread that once a month."

———⬧———

CLEVER TACTICS/ADVICE ON RAISING YOUR MAN
TO ACHIEVE AT OR ABOVE THE EXPECTED LEVEL

1. Before he leaves the house, tell him you're not feeling well and need a solid night's sleep.

2. Never lose it in front of his friends. Ask him if you can have a minute alone. You don't want to seem like the bitch girlfriend/wife.

3. Tell him it's okay, as long as his friends are out in thirty minutes. Surely you can deal for thirty minutes.

4. Buy a noise machine. They really work.

5. Remind him your house isn't an after-hours club.

TIME FOR THE RELATIONSHIP
REPORT CARD!
(Feel Free to Mail This to Your Guy!)

Does he accept responsibility for his actions?

A   B   C   D

Does he accept correction from you?

A   B   C   D

Does he play and work well with others?

A   B   C   D

Does he organize self, materials, and belongings?

A   B   C   D

Does he follow established rules and routines?

A   B   C   D

Comments . . .

PART THREE

Physical Sciences

———

Door Opening/Chores/Sex/Being Sick

Nearly nine out of ten Canadians report that they would be more
attracted to an average-looking person with great manners
than a good-looking person with poor manners.
ANGUS REID STUDY, 2010

CHAPTER TWENTY-FOUR

Hello?
I'm RIGHT BEHIND YOU!

———

The same boyfriend who wrote, "I can't live without you" (hand-written . . . on paper!) certainly seemed to be able to live with giving me concussions. Because that's what happened—or had the potential to happen—every time we walked in or out of someplace with a door. It was as if the man who couldn't live without me always forgot that I was right there behind him. "Thanks," I said on more than one occasion, hoping he'd get the point. "Nothing wakes me up more, or makes me happier, than getting slammed in the face with a glass door!" He got the point—until the next time we entered or exited a door. You don't realize how many doors you enter or exit until you are in a relationship with a man who is not a door-opener. Trust me, doors are constantly being slammed in your face! Good manners are really just a highly evolved form of laziness, I think. So either my boyfriend was completely lazy or he had no manners. (Or maybe it was a bit of both.)

Other women hate when their partners walk so much faster than them, so they're practically chasing them. "I tell him we're just on a nice romantic stroll and he's walking at a pace that I'm practically jogging to keep up," says one of my friends, who likes to take nightly strolls with her boyfriend.

Another friend says that her boyfriend would always leave her to fend for herself when it rained. "If we parked somewhere, he would race out of the car and say, 'I'll meet you in there!' So romantic, right? Or if it was snowing and cold outside, he'd do the same thing. I was like, 'You could wait for me and wrap your arms around me!'"

This also falls under the category of cluelessness when it comes to basic gentlemanly manners. "Once with my boyfriend, we went to look at his new house, which was in the process of being gutted," says one of my friends.

"There was rubble everywhere and I was in heels, because I always wear heels. He didn't notice, or he couldn't care less about my safety. It wasn't very polite, to say the least. He never looked behind to see if I was okay. And I really wasn't. Every step I took, I was worried I was about to wipe out. Still, he was hot as hell," she says. But she dumped him. She couldn't handle that he was so clueless, no matter how sexy he was.

GUEST APPEARANCE FROM A REAL-LIFE EX OF MINE!

"We're not thinking of you all the time," says the ex who always forgot to hold doors open for me and ran across streets, seemingly forgetting that I was with him. "It's a very confusing culture. Do women want us to open the door for them? Will they think we're more of a man, or less of one? Also, these things—like walking beside you, opening car doors—are endless. Guys have spent far more of their lives opening doors just for themselves and walking at their own pace. Then they get married or find themselves in a serious relationship, and now, for the rest of our lives, we have to open the door for someone else?" (Is this the lamest excuse you've ever heard?)

A WORD FROM A GRADE-A HUSBAND . . .

"I'd say that 95 percent of being a good boyfriend or husband, aside from being faithful, is simple things. You can't make us taller. You can't make us better looking. You can't make us funnier. But you can raise us about opening doors. At first, I honestly would forget, and it sounds lame, but I just figured that if any woman was more than four feet away from me, then someone else would open the door for her. Now if I forget, I apologize. It's like the low-hanging fruit. It's right there. Do it and you'll get a lot of points. Because opening the door falls under the Easy Stuff to keep a woman happy. And the Easy Stuff is so easy." (Amen to that!)

WISE WORDS FROM HELENA.
She Does My Brazilian Bikini Waxes. She Knows, Hears, and Sees It All!
"It doesn't bother me. He always carries the heavy stuff for me,
so he's a gentleman in that way. I can open my own door."
(Again, Helena can be so damn reasonable.)

CLEVER TACTICS/ADVICE ON RAISING YOUR MAN TO ACHIEVE AT OR ABOVE THE EXPECTED LEVEL

1. Stand inside until he comes back and opens the door. Eventually, he'll realize you're not with him.

2. Same for the car. Don't get out until he waits for you. Eventually, he'll realize you're not with him.

3. Is it a big deal to you? Maybe not. Choose your battles. Maybe you don't mind opening your own door.

4. Remind him that he loves you, and if he loves you, then he won't want you to get hit by a car (because he'll end up feeling really, really guilty).

CHAPTER TWENTY-FIVE

Use the Button
If You Want
to Turn Me On

T his is a funny joke passed on from an eighty-eight-year-old man to his son, one of my male friends, who passed it on to me. You know it's going to be good, because it's from a man who has been married for almost sixty years! This man told his son, "When you go to bed at night with your girlfriend or wife, hand her two Advils. If she says, 'But I don't have a headache,' then you know she has no excuse not to have sex with you." Ha! It's kind of funny, right? I'm not going to lie. We women do use the headache line when we're tired and don't feel like having sex. (Warning: If your husband hands you two Advils out of the blue one night, take them if you don't feel like having sex.) However, even when we are too tired, we are aware that once we get into it, we're probably going to enjoy it. But some of us, because we're also raising our boyfriends, know why we're so tired: it's because we're also mothers to our men. It's exhausting!

This is why one of my married friends, every time she goes on vacation with her husband, moans, "I guess I'll have to have sex with him." I don't know whether to laugh or cry when she says this to me. They go away together only once (maybe twice) a year. Does that mean they have sex only once (or twice) a year? She really does not want to have sex with her husband. Why? Because he never compliments her, never makes any arrangements for their vacations, doesn't do any chores around the house. Is it any wonder that on her vacation, she really just wants to sleep and *not* have sex with him? But I don't want to think about her sex life, or lack of sex life. I've got my own issues.

Interestingly, most of my married girlfriends, aside from the one mentioned above, are the ones who seem to want it more than their husbands. "At the beginning of our marriage, we would have sex ten or twelve times a week," says one of my girlfriends. (What???) "We'd do it sometimes twice a day," she says. (What???) "But after we had kids, I would always want it more. I would go upstairs first and say, 'You should come up if you want some!' He wouldn't come up. He'd just sit and watch sports." So what happened when he didn't come up? "I just thought, 'I guess we'll go another day and another day without sex,'" she sighs.

The standards you set for sex at the beginning of a relationship (every night, or in my friend's case, twelve times a week!) are hard to keep up. Once the rose-coloured glasses come off, you realize that you can't stay in bed all day because you'll probably be fired.

The question I ask myself when I don't really feel like doing it is, "Do I want to take one for the team?" Or do you just do it when both people want to do it? Hmmmm. Let's take a second and think about it.

Also, I've learned, women don't speak up when their partners don't please them. One of my friends was in a relationship for three years, and her partner could never find her clitoris. She was reluctant to say anything, so she was rubbed dry—literally. And it was far from enjoyable. In fact, it was so *not* enjoyable. One of my other friends recently had a "chat" with her husband. For most of their married life—almost a decade now—they usually had sex three times a week. That number went down until it was only once a week. "I said to him, 'We're not a once-a-week couple, are we?'" she tells me. Her husband responded, "We are definitely not a once-a-week couple. We're a three-times-a-week couple. I'm sorry I've been so tired and busy."

I've talked to both women and men about their sex lives. Funnily enough, men want to be pursued and so do women. So if the man doesn't pursue the woman, then the woman won't pursue the man. And if the woman doesn't pursue the man, then the man won't pursue the woman. Which means there's an awful lot of sex not happening. Don't you find this sad?

GUEST APPEARANCE FROM A
REAL-LIFE EX OF MINE!

This one ex and I had chemistry. I don't remember not wanting to have sex with him, unless I was really sick or had my period. But I wanted to hear his thoughts, because I know he enjoyed sex so much, on couples in relationships when the woman wants more than the man or vice versa. "I remember a specific night you didn't want to have sex," he said. I remember that night too. I told him, "We had sex twice that night!" He responded, "Yes, but you didn't want it a third time." (Okay, maybe he wasn't the best person to ask, but his brain is fascinating to me.)

A WORD FROM A GRADE-A HUSBAND . . .

"Sex is about intimacy, but intimacy is not always about sex. Sometimes my wife and I will both be cuddled under the same blanket on the couch and each reading our own books. Our feet will be touching. I feel like that in itself is like love making. It's just so perfect."

―――――

CLEVER TACTICS/ADVICE ON RAISING YOUR MAN
TO ACHIEVE AT OR ABOVE THE EXPECTED LEVEL

1. Sometimes, you have to be the aggressor. If you want it that bad, you can do this! Just do it! (I find that opening the door in underwear in high heels pretty much shows what you want, without having to say it.)

2. Say straight up: I want some. It's clear. It's concise. There's no reading in between the lines.

3. Surprise him: If you generally don't like morning sex, and he does, start purring in the morning. You'll make his day, and his appreciation will come back in some other form.

4. Remind yourself that you do like sex. Even if you're bored with your partner, or he wants it more, you still like it. Remind yourself that once you get into it, you'll enjoy it. Kind of like going to the dentist. You hate going, but you feel great about it afterwards.

CHAPTER TWENTY-SIX

Just a Little Bit About Porn . . .

N ewsflash: A lot of guys like porn. Shocking, I know. Some women might find it annoying. "I used to care, but now I don't. They're guys," says one of my friends. "If it doesn't interfere with our sex life, then it's okay. It's not always bad unless it impacts your relationship." I agree with this. (You may not, but that's okay. We all have our own opinions.)

JUST A LITTLE BIT ABOUT
NIGHT VERSUS MORNING SEX . . .

And of course, there's the issue of morning sex versus night sex. If you're lucky, you and your partner will be on the same page. You'll both prefer morning sex. Or you'll both prefer night sex. Or, ideally, you'll like both. But usually, I find, men love it in the morning. Women love coffee in the morning. Some women love morning sex, but I'll make a sweeping generalization and say that women like coffee more in the morning. "When we first started dating, we'd have both morning and night sex," says one of my friends. "Now that we have two children, we seem to have sex more in the morning. But it's not as good. It's always rushed. And also, I prefer night sex because his breath is always so bad in the morning. But of course, by nighttime I'm usually too exhausted to have sex."

Also, let's be honest: morning sex is kind of difficult. It's hard for a man when he's hard in the morning to cum when he also has to pee. I'm just saying. (I'm so glad I'm not a guy!)

JUST A LITTLE BIT ABOUT
LIGHTS ON VERSUS LIGHTS OFF . . .

If I'm having drunk sex, I don't mind the lights on. That's because I'm drunk. But if I'm having sober sex (which is 99 percent of the time), I like to have the lights off. "If they're good-looking, you want the lights on," says one of my male friends. "But most women are so self-conscious that they always want the lights off." Maybe it's in our DNA. Or maybe if we got more compliments, we wouldn't be as self-conscious and then would like the lights on. Now, because I know most men do like the lights on, I will compromise. I'm not saying I got a dimmer because of this, but I do have a dimmer because of this. So, gals, get a dimmer. I also know that if you throw a towel or a sheet over your lamp, the light changes . . . in a good way. Especially if the towel or sheet is red. Everyone always looks better in red light. Just my tip to you, my friends.

JUST A LITTLE BIT ABOUT CUDDLING . . .

"You never cuddle with me after we have sex," I said to my boyfriend. I'm not sure I really cared all that much, because he was really bony and it kind of hurt to lie on him, but I did care that he didn't seem to *want* to cuddle.

"Of course I like to cuddle with you," he told me.

"For, like, three seconds, and then you lie on your back and fall asleep," I responded.

"Yes, but I did cuddle, didn't I?" (I suppose three seconds does count.) One of my friends also never gets cuddles after sex. "He sweats so much and says he's always so hot after. So I get about three seconds too."

Also, it's nice to spoon. I like the spoon. I'm not saying you have to spoon me all night, because it *is* kind of hard to sleep like that, but it would be nice to spoon for more than three seconds. How about twenty seconds?

I Just Saved You $200 and Forty-five Minutes of Your Time (Total: $2,800)

I ask Freud about his patients and what they talk about when it comes to sex. "The most common stance is coming from ignorance. One partner craves sexual activity more than the other. It's not gender-biased. For one partner, once a week is enough. For the other, three times a week is good. So someone feels inadequate. The partner who wants it three times a week feels inadequate because they think they should want it less. The other feels inadequate because they think they should want it more. The goal is to NOT take it personally," he says. He tells the story of one husband who always watched porn before he got it on with his wife. Since he had already released (maybe more than once), their love making would last a very, very long time. Too long for her liking.

"People don't want to talk about it. But really they should. They should talk about it over coffee," says Freud. Really? Over coffee? How weird is that? Also, Freud says, don't forget to praise your man. We all know that the ultimate insult to a guy is to tell him he has a small penis. For a man, it's also insulting to hear from his gal, "I'm not going to cum."

Guest Appearance from a Real-Life Ex of Mine!

I've never lost interest in sex with any of my boyfriends. This is probably to do with the fact that we didn't spend every night together, or possibly it's because I like sex and they did too. And usually always, I had great sexual chemistry with my boyfriends. (We may have been sexually compatible, but that didn't meant we were compatible in many other ways, so don't be jealous.) But I asked one ex, who's straight up, what it means when a guy doesn't want to have sex with his wife or girlfriend for a long time. "It means they're not sexually engaged with them anymore." (Okay. Ouch.)

CLEVER TACTICS/ADVICE ON RAISING YOUR MAN
TO ACHIEVE AT OR ABOVE THE EXPECTED LEVEL

1. It's hard, but have the discussion about how much you want it!

2. Surprise him in a sexy outfit.

3. Ask him what he likes, and tell him what you like.

4. I still believe that sometimes you should take one for the team. Likewise, tell him he should take one for the team. I mean, who doesn't feel closer after sex?

CHAPTER TWENTY-SEVEN

The Dishwasher Is NOT Invisible, You Know

W hen I was in my twenties (before I cared if a man was raised or not), I lived with a man for almost two years. Our biggest relationship problem was not that he worked nights and I was at school during the day, but that I was a slob. He was too, but less of one. (I will admit, I was not fully raised myself when it came to cleaning up until I became a mother.) Anyway, we would fight all the time about my sloppiness. My mother's advice was for us to hire a cleaning lady. Now, I didn't have any money in college, but of course, you always have money if you just give something up. Hiring a cleaning lady literally saved our relationship. (Well, not in the long run, but it did help us stay together longer than we would have.) But men *never* seem to learn to clean up after themselves.

"In four years, I don't think my husband has opened the dishwasher," my friend says, sounding dumbfounded. "It just doesn't make any sense." Like so many women I've heard stories from, she can't figure out why her husband takes his dirty dishes over to the sink but somehow can't make the effort to open the

HOW IT GOES WITH MY SIX-YEAR-OLD . . .

"Excuse me! Did you just throw your dirty clothes on the floor?" I'll say.

"Yes," my daughter will respond (laughing).

"Well, where do they go?" I'll press.

"In the laundry," she'll say, grinning.

"Right," I'll say.

She'll pick up her clothes and put them in the hamper.

"And you forgot about your underwear!"

"Okay," she responds, picking up her underwear and putting it in the laundry.

dishwasher RIGHT BESIDE IT. "I've told him now that the kids are getting older that he has to put it into the dishwasher, because they're watching him," she says.

What is it with men and dishes? How can a guy make a bowl of cereal, eat that cereal, and then leave that bowl on the counter when the dishwasher is right there? Well, it's beyond most women.

Another friend moans, "He never cleans up a little bit at a time. He'll never pick up after himself, so when we do decide to clean up, it takes hours. I try telling him that instead of just throwing off his pants every day and leaving them on the floor when he comes home from work, it would be easier to clean up if he did it immediately."

Now that I'm in my thirties and most of my friends are married, I notice that their number-one complaint is that their husbands don't chip in with the housework. One of my friends says, "All he does is take out the trash on Sunday nights. That's *all* he does."

When you have children, the chore division becomes worse. Not only do you have to worry about picking up after yourself, but now there's a third (and maybe fourth or fifth) person you also have to pick up after. (Trust me, if your guy has a problem cleaning up or sharing the chores, it will only get worse once you have a real baby. Not one woman I know who became a mother will tell you otherwise. You will never hear, "After we had our baby, the house became cleaner." Ever.)

My daughter's father lives in another city, and I realize that most of my married friends live pretty much the same way I do. We all end up doing mostly everything that we don't want to do. That's why they're called chores. My daughter can make quite the mess. Come over to our house after a weekend, and you'll think we've been robbed. That's because no one can keep up with a six-year-old. But we try. I damn well make her pick up her stuff. Why? I don't like seeing crayons and markers and papers all over the house. Men, it seems, have what I like to describe as Male Eyes. They don't notice things like dirty dishes or laundry. Or if they do, they don't know what to do about it. One of my friends hates it that her house can be in complete disarray, with dirty dishes piled on the counter, toys strewn everywhere, laundry piled up and needing to be washed and folded, etc. Her husband will stand there and say, "What can I do?" She says, "I feel like yelling, 'OPEN YOUR EYES!' Can men not see what needs to be done? Why do they need us to tell them what needs to be done when it's so very clear what needs to be done?"

"Whenever I come down hard on my husband for not picking up after himself," another friend says, "he'll always say, 'I'm sorry, but I'm used to living on my own.' I'll be like, 'We've lived together for five years now! FIVE YEARS ago you were living on your own. But now it's FIVE YEARS later, and you haven't lived on your own for five years!'"

Another friend gets annoyed because her husband always leaves empty bags of cookies. "I'll find three bags with one cookie left in each. It drives me nuts. It takes up cupboard space, but also, why the hell isn't he eating that last cookie?" (What the hell do they do in the washroom for so long?)

Now that I'm in my thirties, I've realized that no matter how much women have achieved, in a relationship there are PINK JOBS and BLUE JOBS.

PINK JOBS
Doing laundry
Cleaning the washroom
Cleaning the fridge
Writing the grocery list
Making sure the house is stocked

BLUE JOBS
Fixing things
Carrying the groceries inside
Cleaning the snow off cars
Filling the gas tank
Taking out the garbage
Changing light bulbs

That's just the way it is. So there! What are your Pink versus Blue Jobs in your relationship? Post the list on your fridge.

GUEST APPEARANCE FROM A
REAL-LIFE EX OF MINE!

"When you asked why I left the box out after I made myself a bowl of cereal, you were asking as if there was an answer," my ex said. I nagged him more than once about putting the cereal box back where it lives (in the cupboard). "For men, there is no answer. Once we've eaten the cereal, the cereal box doesn't exist. It's done." He also laughed and said, "We know someone else will do it." (Because I'm dating this man while writing this book, he also added, "Besides, *you* left the cereal box out this morning!" Okay. Fine. Whatever. You leave it out way more than I do. *Ha!*)

WISE WORDS FROM HELENA.
She Does My Brazilian Bikini Waxes. She Knows, Hears, and Sees It All!
"Are you kidding me? Do you think most of my clients are married to saints?
I don't think most of my clients' boyfriends or husbands know where the sink is!
My husband will say, 'I'll do it later.' But later turns into much later.
And I think he thinks the whole house is his closet. I just tell him, 'Do you ever
have to pick up my clothes? So have the same courtesy for me.' But he can cook!"
(Helena looks at the bright side of things. We can and should learn from her!)

CHAPTER TWENTY-EIGHT

Why Separating Whites and Darks Can Lead to a Different Kind of Separation

I have to write a brief paragraph about laundry. Men hate laundry, but guess what? So do women! (Aside from my friend Joanna, that is, who loves doing laundry because she loves the fresh smell of clean laundry and the sight of neatly folded clothes.) One of my friends, when I asked her why she got divorced, said, "For ten years, all we fought about was the laundry. I told him practically from the minute I got pregnant that since I had carried the baby, it was now his job to do the laundry." So did her husband do it? "He would do it, but not all of it." Frankly, I find this story a little odd but somewhat hilarious. They didn't get divorced because someone cheated. They didn't get divorced because they weren't into each other anymore. They got divorced because of laundry! "Our marriage," she says again, "really did dissolve over the laundry." Strange but true. (I'm not making this shit up!) Consider this a warning.

GUEST APPEARANCE FROM A REAL-LIFE EX OF MINE!

When I ask why he never cleaned up after himself, my ex answers curtly, "I always had my mother who put shit away for me." (He has a way with words, doesn't he?)

A WORD FROM A GRADE-A HUSBAND . . .

"When I was in college, that was when I first realized about keeping neat. Sorry, we were in a dorm of all men. We never changed the bed sheets; we never showered. I was lucky if I brushed my teeth. But then I met a girl who wouldn't sleep with me until I changed my sheets. That did it. But now, I know I just suck at chores. I'd rather throw off my pants on a Friday night and get into them on Saturday. I PREFER it. I don't know why. I throw money at that problem and pay for a cleaning lady to come twice a week. And really, if I need something and have to do laundry, I do it. Laundry may be boring, but it's the easiest thing in the world to do."

CLEVER TACTICS/ADVICE ON RAISING YOUR MAN TO ACHIEVE AT OR ABOVE THE EXPECTED LEVEL

1. Tell him that if he leaves clothes on the floor, they're going in the garbage.

2. Tell him you think he's man enough to open the dishwasher.

3. Make a deal that if you cook, he has to clean up. You too have to follow this rule.

4. Tell him the tale of the couple who got DIVORCED over laundry! Do you want to be the couple who gets divorced over laundry?

5. Cut back on something and get a cleaning person. (Throw $ at the problem.)

6. Make a big sign with the words "THIS IS THE DISHWASHER" and tape it to the dishwasher.

CHAPTER TWENTY-NINE

Diagnosis?
Man Cold.
Prescription?
Shut the Fuck Up

———

I once went on a blind date with a man who picked me up in a fancy convertible, had picked out the restaurant, and seemed like a smart, nice guy (who was also employed). On paper, he was good. He had taken the initiative by asking me out, picking me up, and choosing the restaurant. Unfortunately, I realized after sitting down across from him for less than ten minutes that he was kind of a baby. I figured out quite quickly that he would not be good at being sick, because he wasn't even sick and he was complaining about his health (at age thirty-six). The waiter had asked if he wanted a drink. He ordered water. After the waiter left, my date explained that he had allergies. He went on . . . and on . . . and on . . . and on about his allergies. That's right. Bottoms up! (I needed to drink!) He was allergic to trees, and flowers, and cats and dogs, he told me. I was allergic to him, I thought, trying to stifle my yawns.

Once, another man got angry with me for not treating him like a dying man when he had a bad stomach for a night. He sent me an e-mail saying I should have said, "Jeez, so sorry to hear you're not feeling well. Hope you're feeling better soon. Take care. Have a bowl of soup and go to bed early. We'll talk later." When I didn't respond, he wrote, "Would you like all the details, including a 4 p.m. Saturday to 10 a.m. Sunday chronic burping session? (You can't fall asleep when you are burping, I've learned.) Or the sweating? Or the lack of food? Or the dehydration? I won't bother bringing up what went on in my bathroom over the last couple of days. That's kind of obvious."

Well, there's nothing like being a single working mother to learn what being sick is really like. I once was so sick that I took myself to the hospital, and still I managed to pick my daughter up from school at 3 p.m.

The Man Cold, as my friend calls it, is the worst. "They act like they're *dying*," she says. "It's just a cold!"

"OH, MY GOD," says another friend about her husband. "He gets a stuffed nose and it's the end of the world and he has to stay in bed. He'll say, 'I can't do anything. I'm sick.' And to make matters worse, he also has bad allergies, so every time it was allergy season, he'd whine and complain about being up all night. I'm like, 'Shut up, baby. Go have a C-section and then talk to me.' I would bring him tea, but through gritted teeth. I would try to be nice while thinking, 'You are such a fucking baby.' Meanwhile, when I'm sick, he'll very rarely come up to bring me tea or check on me. Then again, I don't really have the option of being sick, because I'm a mother."

GUEST APPEARANCE FROM A
REAL-LIFE EX OF MINE!

I asked an ex why men act like babies when they have a cold. "It's the Mommy Syndrome. All men are little boys when they are sick. We want to be cared for," he tells me. And he was sick. A lot. He seemed to get sick every other week. "Studies have shown that men feel pain more than women. Women go through childbirth, so their threshold for pain is higher," he continues. "Also, men are filled with self-pity. Women are tougher." (Screw you! Why should we be punished because we're tougher?)

A WORD FROM A GRADE-A HUSBAND . . .

"I never get sick," my friend's husband says. (OMG!!! Don't you just love this guy?)

CLEVER TACTICS/ADVICE ON RAISING YOUR MAN TO ACHIEVE AT OR ABOVE THE EXPECTED LEVEL

1. Remind him that you gave birth, or one day will give birth—that you had a baby come out of your VAGINA!

2. Baby him a little. But not too much. Find the fine line.

3. Remind him that he's a *man*.

4. Put him on a daily regimen of vitamin C.

5. Dress in a sexy nurse's outfit. Turn him on! Men do seem to forget about their sickness when they know they're going to get laid.

6. If #5 works, tell him he was healthy enough to have sex, so he should get the hell out of bed!

CHAPTER THIRTY

Why Male Nurses Are Sexy... Or So We Think

I hadn't heard from a good friend in almost a week. "I'm getting worried," I texted her. "Send me an e-mail just to let me know you're alive." She finally called. She sounded like she had been run over by a truck. "I've been in bed all week," she croaked. "I couldn't even get out of bed. I had to send my kids to my parents'."

"Oh, my God," I said. "You could have called me. Where was your husband?"

"He was so awful," she moaned. "I literally couldn't get out of bed. He was home and I would send him an e-mail begging him to go out and get me ginger ale."

Another friend's husband never believes her when she's sick. "I literally will have to prove it to him. He'd say, 'Do you really need to stay in bed?' I'd go to the doctor and come home with a prescription for bronchitis and then he'd be like, 'Okay, maybe you should be in bed.' But on weekends, even if I was sick, I *couldn't* be sick. I'd have to be with the kids."

One of my friends tells me a story that I have to preface by saying THIS REALLY HAPPENED. "I had to go to the hospital, and I called my husband and he said he couldn't miss an important meeting. My dad took me. When I left [for home again], I called my husband and he said his meeting was just about to start. I literally walked home. When I got home, I found him in the garage smoking a cigarette like he was a teenager and had just been caught. He told me his meeting had been cancelled at the last minute. I was like, 'So why didn't you call me and come pick me up?'" (Seriously. I'm not making this shit up!)

A Word from a Grade-A Husband . . .

"When a woman is sick, that's like striking gold! You make her chicken soup. Taking care of your wife or girlfriend when she's sick falls under the 'good husband' column. Plus, it's fun to nurture someone. And the gratitude?"

———————◆———————

WISE WORDS FROM HELENA. She Does My Brazilian Bikini Waxes. She Knows, Hears, and Sees It All!

"If I say I have a headache, my husband will say his elbow hurts. If I say my back hurts, he'll say he's in pain all over the place. I can't be in pain or sick without him being in more pain or more sick. All my female clients moan about this. These are women who get sick and can still go to work, take care of their children, do the laundry, make dinner. With men? I don't know. What is up with that when they get sick?" (Good question, Helena. Good question.)

———————◆———————

CLEVER TACTICS/ADVICE ON RAISING YOUR MAN TO ACHIEVE AT OR ABOVE THE EXPECTED LEVEL

1. Show him the doctor's note!

2. Act very grateful when he does take care of you. Tell him you'll owe him one.

3. Bring in back-up, like your parents. Nothing like having in-laws around to get your guy to step up his game.

CHAPTER THIRTY-ONE

Help in Aisle Five!
There's a Clueless Man
Grocery Shopping

S o of course, you all know by know about my Grocery Store Incident
(where my boyfriend ditched me at the checkout with a cart so
overflowing with food, I could barely push it). Men at all stages of
a relationship, it seems, need help when it comes to grocery shopping. Even if they do go grocery shopping, they still need extra help.

"I give him jobs," my friend says. Since they had their first child, just
over six months ago, her husband's job has been to shop on Saturday
mornings. Which is nice of him. "But he goes to three stores. He'll go to
Costco. He'll go to Loblaws, and he'll go to another store in our area. We
get, literally, the same things every week. Every single week, the list never
changes. What takes me twenty minutes to get takes him three hours!"

Another friend moans that while her husband will go grocery shopping,
he never looks at prices. "He always just buys the most expensive things.
I asked him to buy baking soda, just plain baking soda so I could bake a
cake, and he comes back with the most expensive, individually wrapped
packages of baking soda. Or if we need ketchup? Forget about him buying
the big plastic bottle like the rest of the world. He'll buy two small glass
bottles instead, because they look fancier."

Another friend's live-in boyfriend is an "impulse" buyer. "We need basic
things and suddenly he comes home with these frozen yogurt things. We
don't eat yogurt. He doesn't eat yogurt. I swear to God, one day he'll come
home with dog food. We don't own a dog!" Then she's forced to return things.

It was nearly impossible for me to find one woman who didn't complain
about men and grocery shopping. "I do a detailed list for my husband.

I literally write out, 'Grab a cart, grab a coffee.' And, 'This is what is in aisle one; this is in aisle two.' I have to," she explains. "I have to be as detailed as possible." Still, even her detailed directions don't always work. "He'll somehow manage to forget my yogurt, which is what I eat for breakfast every day, and yet he remembers his cereal."

Other women know they have to be detailed too when they send their husbands or boyfriends grocery shopping. "I have learned that I can't just write down 'soap.' Even though we have been using the same brand of unscented soap for four years, if I write down 'soap,' he'll end up coming home with some scented brand that I've never heard of."

Other women wonder if grocery stores bring on adult ADD. One of my friends is hilarious when she talks about her husband and the grocery store. "His attention span is, like, zero," she says. "So even if I write only ten things on the list, I know I'll only get the first five. So whenever I do a grocery list, I really have to think about it very carefully. I need to be cautious of what we really need and make sure I get them in the top five on the list."

Also, men do disappear in grocery stores. "My boyfriend is the worst when we go grocery shopping together," says another friend. "I swear, he'll be right beside me and I'll reach up to grab a box of crackers, and then I'll look beside me and he's gone. He's just vanished, like into thin air. It's the oddest thing. But it pisses me off. I'm like, 'I looked up for TWO SECONDS and you've taken off. And now it's going to take me twenty minutes to find you.'"

Some of my female friends are constantly raising their husbands, like they do their children. "I now warn my husband. As we're walking into the grocery story, I tell him, 'We're not in a rush. We have nothing to do after this. I want to take my time here.'" My friend has been forced to talk to her husband like he's a child because of past shopping excursions. They'd walk in, and before she had even put three items into the cart, he'd be at the checkout counter, waiting for her impatiently.

Another friend refuses to take her husband grocery shopping now. She wants to get in and out. But her husband would get in hour-long discussions about the meat with the deli guy.

I will mention that there are *some* women who detest grocery shopping so much that they will say that their favourite thing about their husband is that he'll grocery shop. "Sometimes I'll be so mad at him about something," says one woman. "But I hate grocery shopping. And then he'll do it, and I'll remember how much I love him." (She's the only one I found!)

A Word from a Grade-A Husband . . .

"I did have to learn in this department," he admits. "Guys just don't have the imagination for groceries. A guy will just buy ten items. If they feel like pasta, they'll buy ten packages of pasta and five bags of chips. Also, I had to really pay attention, because I didn't know what baking soda is. I didn't know what vanilla extract is. But I've learned. My wife has opened my eyes to a whole new world when it comes to grocery shopping. When I first got married, it really did bring me such joy. I really was enthralled by how women look at stuff and what they can find on the shelf."

CLEVER TACTICS/ADVICE ON RAISING YOUR MAN TO ACHIEVE AT OR ABOVE THE EXPECTED LEVEL

1. When you make a list, make sure you really think about it. Because men do have ADD when they grocery shop.
2. Tell him to buy himself a treat, like Fruit Loops.
3. Take turns grocery shopping.
4. Make it a game. Tell him you want to see how fast he can do it. Make a bet, even. Whoever can do it faster wins something.

5. Remind him that you don't have a dog, so you don't need dog food.

6. Remember, guys really don't know what baking powder or vanilla extract is. So lower your expectations a bit and take the time to explain.

7. Forget the stuff he likes and ask him how it feels when you come home without his cereal.

CHAPTER THIRTY-TWO

The Needy Guy
(Stop the Madness!)

O ne man I dated was super needy . . . in a really odd way. But it turns out that he wasn't unique in what he needed. I'm talking about the male massage. "Oh, I hate when guys ask you to give them a massage," moans one of my single girlfriends. "Guys who want massages all the time are the worst." Now, I do give arm tickles to my six-year-old to help her fall asleep. But I'm her mother. I need her to fall asleep. I love her. So I don't mind tickling her arm. But this guy would place his arm on my stomach. He liked the arm tickle too. (I should have taken this as a warning.) So I would tickle his arm . . . for twenty minutes. The second I stopped, he would shake his arm, telling me without words to carry on. I couldn't take it. I found it so unattractive.

Guess what? A friend of mine had an even worse experience with a needy guy. Her needy guy was a powerful banker by day. At night, he liked her to sing him lullabies. Yes! Lullabies! He was thirty-five! Need I say more? (Okay, you can stop laughing. Okay, you can continue laughing. It's entirely true and so funny.) Talk about the neediest of all needy guys! Suddenly the guy who wanted the arm tickle doesn't look so bad. (Well, not *as* bad.)

I Just Saved You $200 and Forty-five Minutes of Your Time (Total: $3,000)

"Needy men are insecure and can be scared. When someone is acting needy it's usually because he is scared of something. But everyone is needy sometimes. If a guy is needy in the sense that he wants massages, it's a way of asking you to show how much you care about him. If you love him, you need to understand this, but you also have to keep his neediness contained. Each person in a couple is needy, but you have to make sure your needs are different from your partner's." Meaning, you can't have *two* people in a relationship who *need* foot massages. "Your neediness has to be compatibly different." For example, my guy may need massages, but I *need* phone call checkins. Maybe it all does balance out.

CLEVER TACTICS/ADVICE ON RAISING YOUR MAN TO ACHIEVE AT OR ABOVE THE EXPECTED LEVEL

1. What can I say about a guy who needs to be sung lullabies? Just sing off key!

2. Tickle or massage for ten minutes. Then demand the same treatment.

3. Don't start doing it at all.

4. Get him a gift certificate for a professional massage.

CHAPTER THIRTY-THREE

The Gas Station.
How to Fill Up the Car

L ike many women, I used to be scared of gas stations. I honestly
believed that somehow, I'd blow myself up just by opening
the . . . what's that thing called? Where you put that gas nozzle
thing in? Anyway, gas stations were never a problem when I
was with a man. That's because filling the gas tank is a BLUE job (a man's
job). But after I found myself single for the first time in years, and with an
empty gas tank, I knew I'd have to fill it up myself. First I wondered, "Where
are all the full-service gas stations?" After driving around for nearly an
hour, I still couldn't find one. I had to—gulp—fill it up on my own. So now
I'm not nearly as scared as I once was (though I will admit my heart does
still beat quickly and I can't wait to drive outta there).

Men like gas stations. Or at least, they don't seem to mind getting out of
the car and filling the tank, while you sit in the passenger seat and rest your
feet on the dashboard. In fact, my last boyfriend loved going to the gas
station. He was obsessed about keeping his white Range Rover clean. It got
to the point that I was like, "Do we have to go through the car wash again?"
(Going through a car wash isn't as much fun when you're in your mid-
thirties as it is when you're six!) Anyway, the car wash and going to gas
stations—these were his things.

While men may like gas stations—or at least aren't scared of them—it
does seem like they have a problem actually getting to one for you. They
like SAYING they'll take care of the gas situation. "My husband promised to
get gas in my car, as he always does. On Sunday, I said I would go and
he said, 'I'll take care of it.' He promised. Sure enough, I get into the
car Monday morning, already late to a meeting, and of course there's no
gas in the car."

Men don't understand that we females have no concept of the gas tank. When that light pops on, warning us that we're running low on gas, we really think we need gas RIGHT NOW. We can't get to our next destination without thinking that we are going to run out of gas. That little light coming on freaks us out. Men don't get freaked out when the little light comes on. They don't get freaked out at all. What woman hasn't heard from her mate, "Oh, you could drive out to the country and back and still have enough gas to get to work tomorrow"? My friend's husband is like this. "He'll always say to me, 'Don't worry. You could drive all over town and you'd still be good for two more days.'"

Another friend is annoyed whenever her husband takes on the task of filling up. He does it, but at the gas station, he becomes oddly cheap. "He has this habit of only putting in ten dollars," she laughs, shaking her head sadly. "I'll be like, 'You were at the gas station. Why didn't you just fill it up?' He'll say, 'Because that's all I had on me.' I'm like, 'You do know that they take bank cards and credit cards!'" If you're going to fill up the car, then FILL UP the car.

Another couple I know share a car between them. "From the start, I told him that if we ever run out of gas, we're going to get a divorce," she says. Well, they're still together, so that must mean they've never run out of gas, right? "Even though I was loud and clear about him always having the gas tank full, he would push it. He would *really* push it. That lever would be around empty more often than not. Even the threat of DIVORCE didn't seem to faze him."

CLEVER TACTICS/ADVICE ON RAISING YOUR MAN
TO ACHIEVE AT OR ABOVE THE EXPECTED LEVEL

1. Driving with a maniac boyfriend or husband is a great time to practice your meditation and yoga breathing. Think of it that way. See how far you're coming along in your practice?

2. Bring your own earphones and music in the car. Put them in your ears. Tell him you prefer to listen to the soothing tones of (fill in musician) than his screaming and honking. He'll either get the hint, and quiet down, or you'll get to listen to some music you love. It's win-win, either way.

3. Remind him he's not in a rush. Tell him that you "enjoy" every second with them, even in the car, so why is he rushing? Say it with a sweet smile. Who can resist how sweet you are!

4. If they promise to put in gas, and you know there's a chance they'll forget, stick a sign on your car window that says, "I need gas!" Do it three days before you actually really need gas.

CHAPTER THIRTY-FOUR

You're "Driving" Me Insane! This Should Not Be the Highway to Hell!

I s it just me or are many men not fun in cars? In fact, driving in a big city is stressful enough without the guy who supposedly loves you yelling, "Get in that lane. No, the other lane! Why did you get in this lane? Go in the other lane!" And, "You could have made that light! Why are you driving so slow?" Okay, I admit that sometimes I drive like a senior citizen. I don't rush through yellow lights. One of my exes hated this. "You could have made that light!" he'd always moan, at every single light. And I'd say, "So we could save what? A whole thirty seconds? Where are we rushing to?"

With men who like to lane change, I always find myself wanting to yell, "It doesn't matter what friggin lane we're in. It's rush hour!" Again, even if I had switched lanes, we would have saved a whole thirty seconds. I finally said to each of them, "You know why I drive so slowly with you? Because I like spending time with you. Even in the car." That shut them up.

"We get into fights all the time when we drive together and he's driving. He's a honker, for one thing. If some other driver does the tiniest thing wrong, he'll have to honk at them. Not only will he have to honk at them, but he'll have to drive up and glare at whoever is driving. He also starts up with people. I will yell at him, 'Could you not when I'm in the car? Do it on your own time.' I'll tell him, 'You don't know if they have a bat or gun in their car.' There have been a few times when it looked like he would be getting into a fight. And I'd be like, 'You started that!'"

Another friend literally screams when she drives with her husband. Now they take two cars to their cottage because of his driving. "I know he's a skilled driver, but he drives like a maniac. He loves to weave lanes and I can't stand it. I used to scream, but now I just take another car if we're going away to the cottage."

Another friend will hold on for dear life to her seatbelt and put her hands on the dashboard when her husband drives. "My husband knows I'm anxious and scared of getting in an accident, and he'll just say, 'Well, if we wipe out, your hands being out in front of you like that isn't going to help!'" It's true. Most women I know *are* anxious. Maybe it's because we have kids and value our lives. We'd like to get back home to our kids . . . alive.

Some couples don't have cars. One of my friends' husbands, for whatever reason, refuses to sit behind the taxi driver. "We'd be going to a formal event. I'd have this huge ball gown on and I'd have to scooch over."

I also heard the strangest story from a woman who got into a wicked fight with her husband over parking. "We didn't speak, literally, for five days. What happened was that we parked somewhere and we couldn't find the car after. He thought because he drove that I should have paid attention to where we parked. Does that make any sense? When we finally found the car, he was like, 'I don't want to hear one word from you during this car ride.' He was so mad because we couldn't find the car."

I Just Saved You $200 and Forty-five Minutes of Your Time (Total: $3,200)

Freud says that cars have a different meaning for men. In fact, Freud says that cars are an "extension" of a man's penis. (Oh, it's all making sense now.) "Cars are about ego," says Freud.

GUEST APPEARANCE FROM A
REAL-LIFE EX OF MINE!

"Why did I hate when you drove and I was in the car? Because you drive like an eighty-five-year-old. Because you would not ever pass up a chance to hit a red light. Because your musical taste is appalling," my ex ranted when I asked him why he always yelled at me when I drove. "It would save a tremendous amount of effort in a relationship if the guy always drove. Hire a cleaning lady and let a guy drive, and you'll have a good foundation for a relationship." (Oh, so that's the reason we're no longer together.)

CLEVER TACTICS/ADVICE ON RAISING YOUR MAN
TO ACHIEVE AT OR ABOVE THE EXPECTED LEVEL

1. Tell him you value your life, and *his*!

2. Whoever drives gets to choose the music.

3. Tell him that you like being with him, and that's why you're driving so slowly. It's sweet!

4. Remind him you're not in a rush.

5. Remind him often that he *does* have a big penis, and maybe he'll stop thinking the car is an extension of it.

6. Learn how to fill up the gas tank on your own. It really isn't that bad. If I can do it, anyone can. Trust me.

TIME FOR THE RELATIONSHIP
REPORT CARD!
(Feel Free to Mail This to Your Guy!)

Does he use his time productively?

A   B   C   D

Does he participate actively in group activities?

A   B   C   D

Does he demonstrate the appropriate attention span?

A   B   C   D

Does he work independently?

A   B   C   D

Does he stay on task?

A   B   C   D

Does he appropriately complete daily work assignments?

A   B   C   D

Comments . . .

Attitude/Effort

Buying Gifts/Celebrating/Being Supportive

How can a woman be expected
to be happy with a man
who insists on treating her
as if she were a perfectly normal
human being?
OSCAR WILDE

CHAPTER THIRTY-FIVE

Movie Night. What Do You Mean You Don't Want to See The Notebook?

I wondered how I had ended up here. Where was here? I was in line at a movie theatre Burger King, with an order for two chicken sandwiches, three fries, and three Diet Cokes, while my boyfriend was in the actual movie theatre with my daughter. The movie had just started. Why, I wondered, was I in line with a food order like I was a waitress, knowing there was no way I could carry all that shit on my own, while my boyfriend, WHO HAD ALREADY SEEN THE MOVIE, was in the theatre . . . well, watching the movie he had already seen? I had a flash of what should have happened. My boyfriend should have said, "I've already seen the movie. I don't want you to miss the beginning. What do you guys want to eat? I'll go get it."

Another boyfriend would never go to girl movies with me. I sort of understood this, until I got to the theatre and saw men with their wives and girlfriends at their sides. Now to be fair, the men looked sheepish, embarrassed, and not exactly thrilled to be there. But still, they *were* there. One of my female friends, now married, says she's always getting into fights over who gets to pick the movie. In fact, her first major argument with her husband was over picking out a DVD. "He kept persevering. He kept promising I'd love it. I admit I wanted to watch some chick flick. We had a huge argument about it. I just let him pick. My night was ruined. Did I love it? No! It was some horror movie."

One of my friends always got her husband to go to the movie of her choice by saying, "It got the New York Critics Choice Award." He fell for it a number of times before realizing that all the movies sucked. He finally asked her, "Is there such a thing as the New York Critics Choice Award?" My friend looked away sheepishly. She had made it up. "There's no such thing, is there? You totally made that up!" Well, it was nice while it lasted, before she got busted.

Another friend hasn't got to pick the movie in seven years. That's right, *seven years*—ever since she first picked out a movie when she was just dating her now husband. "Oh, my God. I took him to see some movie that was so chick flick. And after, he said, 'That is for sure the last time you're choosing a movie.' He actually said, 'Your movie-choosing privileges have been banned. INDEFINITELY.'"

Trust me, guys are onto us. They have their own negotiating tactics. I know, because I asked a man. "My negotiating tactic is to immediately suggest the most un-girly movie and then compromise. E.g., girl says, 'Want to see *The Notebook*?' I'll say, 'Hmmm. *Predator versus Alien* looks really good.' Girl will say, 'Hmmm. Let's see what else is playing. *Ocean's Thirteen*?' Me: Bingo!'"

Another male friend tells me that once on a first date, the gal suggested they see a movie starring America's sweetheart. He told her, straight up, "I will never see that movie. You can dump me now if you want." That's how serious movie discussions can be in a relationship. This man was willing to have a woman dump him before they even *met*, all because he refused to see a girlie movie.

GUEST APPEARANCE FROM A REAL-LIFE EX OF MINE!

I asked this ex why we always fought about who got to pick the movie. "You always picked shitty movies," he said. "At least they were bombs, so it allowed me to have a full-on rant afterwards. Listen, movies are about taste, what you like and what I like. Ideally, you thought you had found a partner who liked everything you did. This is a terrible mistake women make. It will rarely happen. And I think you felt that if you didn't like the movie I picked, then potentially you were with the wrong mate. And that was a totally wrong way of looking at it. Also, it's a *huge* disappointment for men that women don't like horror movies. Bottom line, women have a higher tolerance than guys for terrible romance movies." (Um . . . I actually don't mind the occasional horror movie. Just sayin'.)

CLEVER TACTICS/ADVICE ON RAISING YOUR MAN TO ACHIEVE AT OR ABOVE THE EXPECTED LEVEL

1. Lie and say that the movie got GREAT reviews from some made-up bullshit movie critic. I think this is brilliant. If you don't get busted.

2. Pick the absolute cheesiest movie (one you don't really want to see) and then pretend you're making a big compromise by choosing something less girly.

3. Promise that if you get to pick the movie this time, he can choose the next one. Keep this promise.

4. Tell him you'll treat him to popcorn. Tell him you'll give him a blow job afterwards.

CHAPTER THIRTY-SIX

You Can Remember Who Won the 1991 World Series, but You Can't Remember Our Anniversary?

"**M**en don't pick up the cues," one married woman I know says. "They miss them. When I say to my husband, 'Oh, isn't that sweet that So-and-so's husband bought her that diamond bracelet for their fifth anniversary?' I'm saying that not just to make conversation. I'm saying that our fifth anniversary is coming up and I want a good gift. That's what I'm saying."

VALENTINE'S DAY

I was shocked to learn one year that I was in a relationship with possibly the one man in North America who did not know that Valentine's Day is on February 14. You did not misread that. My boyfriend did not know that February 14 is Valentine's Day. How could this be? you're probably wondering, as I did. For the past forty years of his life, had he not noticed that every week in February, stores were filled with stuffed bears with hearts that said "I love you" and "Be mine"? Had he not noticed the red balloons everywhere or the advertisements for flowers and special prix fixe menus? Was he that clueless? Yes. Yes. Yes. It was shocking, as well, because he had been married for thirteen years. Did that mean he never celebrated Valentine's Day with his wife? Did that mean his wife was a mute? I don't know any woman who doesn't mention to her boyfriend or husband, "Oh, you know that Valentine's Day is coming up soon."

I don't care, as many men argue, that Valentine's Day is a Hallmark holiday. Get that? I. Don't. Care. I want the day to be acknowledged. I want it to be celebrated. And by celebrated and acknowledged, I mean I want my boyfriend to do *something* to show me that I'm special. So because this guy was so clueless about how to do Valentine's Day, I kept bringing it up, telling him about a bracelet I liked on a website and how easy it was to order it online. I made such a huge deal about the day that I scared him away. He dumped me the day before Valentine's Day. I think the pressure got to him. The day after Valentine's Day, he wanted to get back together. I was just another sad girl on Valentine's Day, another statistic.

"It's like he has the amazing ability just to tune the day out," says one of my married friends, who does not get a thing on Valentine's Day.

BIRTHDAYS

On one of my more recent birthdays, the man I was dating was out of town on business. He of course knew it was my birthday. (Can you tell I'm the type of gal who lets these special days be known?) There was a knock at the door, and when I saw the FedEx man standing there with a parcel, I knew immediately it was from my man. "Yippee!" I thought. "He remembered!"

The delivery man handed over the package.

"Thank you!" I said, excited to rip open the package and see my gift.

"That will be $72.50," he said.

"Sorry?" I asked, confused.

"That will be $72.50. It says, 'Payment on delivery.'"

"It says what?"

"Payment on delivery," he responded. "It's $72.50."

"What?"

I fumbled around every change drawer in my house and came up with the money. The gift was no longer important. The gift, just so you know, cost less than I had paid the delivery man.

Now, though it was thoughtful of my boyfriend to pick something out for me, and it was thoughtful to deliver it to me, it was so thoughtless not to have paid for the delivery. What was up with that?

One of my friends got furious with her husband when he didn't say "Happy birthday." Right before bed, he handed her a gift certificate. "There was no thought to a gift certificate," she complained.

"My last birthday, my boyfriend and I got into a huge fight over dinner," says one of my friends. "I don't remember what it was about, so it must have been that stupid, but I do know he was in a bad mood. So we had three different birthday dinners after that to make up for it. It didn't really make up for it, though."

One of my friends got the worst gifts from her boyfriend. "He once got me a vacuum cleaner. And he got me this gadget that cleans up crumbs," she says. (Again, I'm not making this shit up!) At least she didn't have to pay for the delivery.

MOTHER'S DAY

I know a lot of mothers. Most of my friends are now mothers. But not one of them has managed to have a good Mother's Day. Mother's Day is kind of like New Year's Eve. It's always high expectations, then . . . bust. As a mother, I've tried to train myself not to expect anything. Then it might be better than I hope for (kind of like New Year's Eve). We need to train ourselves to do this.

My friend has probably the funniest/saddest first Mother's Day story. On the eve of the day, she and her husband came home from dinner. After saying goodbye to their nanny, she noticed a dozen roses and a gift bag on the dining-room table. "I thought, 'How sweet of my husband to get me something before the actual day.'" She skipped over to the flowers and opened the gift bag. Inside was a picture frame that read "World's Greatest Mom," featuring a photo of her son. Inside the gift bag was a stack of photos of her son. She opened the card and realized that none of it was from her husband. It was from her *nanny.* "So you'd definitely think my husband would be well aware of the day after seeing that my nanny got me something. And of course, I had mentioned it all week. I mean, come on. Mother's Day is like Christmas now. You know it's coming."

The following morning, she came downstairs. (Her husband did let her sleep in.) Her husband handed her a card. "I opened it and thought he was joking. He didn't even sign it 'Love.' My face fell because I knew that's all there was, and it wasn't a joke. That's all he had planned, and all he was planning, to do." Her husband knew, from her fallen expression, that he had failed miserably, and he stormed off. "I think he was a little humiliated. So I went to the gym and came home and told him, 'I don't want this to turn into a *thing.* Let's just move on with our day.'" They did. They went to her brother's for an early dinner. When they got back home, there was a HUGE bouquet of flowers at her doorstep. "I thought he had made up for it," my friend recounts. "And that while we were at my brother's, he had called and ordered them." She opened the card, which read, "I always feel safe when my children are with you. Thank you for being such a good person." Yup, that's right. Her husband's *ex*-wife had sent my friend flowers. She got two bouquets of flowers that Mother's Day, neither from her husband. "I told him that he *should* really feel bad. Our nanny gets me something and his ex-wife got me something!" (This is why many mothers like their nannies more sometimes than they do their spouses.)

"I'd usually get a card, but he'd never make plans," says another friend. "There was zero thought about Mother's Day. He'd get me a gift certificate every single Mother's Day and Valentine's Day. It would be nice to have one year with a little more thought." Another friend, since day one of her marriage, always had to buy and plan something for Mother's Day. Not for herself but for her husband's mother. "I had to find his mother a Mother's Day gift. It would always be up to me. I'd buy his father a gift for Father's Day. He'd go golfing," she says.

•

The worst? A friend of mine, whose husband was golfing, got a message on her BlackBerry. "Happy Mother's Day," was all it said. She didn't even get a card!

Listen, boys, you know the saying "You only have once chance to make a first impression"? The same goes for our first Mother's Day. As my friend says, "I'm never going to get back my first Mother's Day." (Not that she'd want it, but you get the point.) "Nothing happened on Mother's Day for me," my friend says. "*Nothing* happened. I told him I wanted a bag, so we went purse shopping. But we had our kids with us and they were wild, so I couldn't even look around. We just went home. So when I say nothing happened, I mean it."

Another friend got upset that her husband didn't get her a gift from her son. I get this. For Father's Day, I get my daughter's father a gift from me and also have my daughter make a gift for him. It sounds like we're asking for a lot, but we're not. You just have to understand us.

Cards (There's a Reason Hallmark Does So Well!)

"I look forward to cards," my friend says. "I grew up in a family where we celebrated all the Hallmark holidays." Her boyfriend understands this. She even used to get "dating" cards from him on the anniversary of their first date.

Guest Appearance from a Real-Life Ex of Mine!

"Men don't care as much about gifts. One's expectations never match reality, like a wedding day. Most people are so frantic and overwrought. But men also do like getting gifts for their birthday . . . Wait a minute, did you ever get me a gift?" (Okay, this book is not called *How to Raise a Girlfriend.* Gotta run!)

I Just Saved You $200 and Forty-five Minutes of Your Time (Total: $3,400)

Sometimes I don't like Freud. When I ask him why men are so bad at celebrating or acknowledging special occasions, he says the problem lies with WOMEN. Um, hello? Why am I paying you $200 again? Isn't he supposed to be on *my* side? I listen as he explains that women are the ones who like this kind of attention (duh!), and that women feel the need to remind their men. But once we do remind them, we immediately wonder, "Why do I have to remind you?" So we women are putting too much pressure, and then we still aren't satisfied. (I can't really say anything about this, since I was the one *dumped* because I put too much pressure on my boyfriend before Valentine's Day.) So I get his point. I don't necessarily *like* his point, but I get it. Sometimes Freud is a fucking genius. When I ask him how we ladies can let our men know that a certain day is important to us without having to bash it into their brains, he suggests programming the date into their PDAs. He suggests programming every important date—your birthday, Mother's Day, anniversaries—into their PDAs or telling their assistants. It's pure genius.

WISE WORDS FROM HELENA. She Does My Brazilian Bikini Waxes. She Knows, Hears, and Sees It All!

"I will say my husband is not so great with the gifts. However, I told him at the start of our marriage that I didn't care so much about presents, but I do care about cards, because cards are very important to me. And he's never forgotten that." She also adds that while he might not be so adept at buying gifts, *"he is great at buying me flowers. And he always remembers important dates, like anniversaries and birthdays."* (Again, Helena finds the silver lining!)

CLEVER TACTICS/ADVICE ON RAISING YOUR MAN
TO ACHIEVE AT OR ABOVE THE EXPECTED LEVEL

1. Do break into his BlackBerry to plug in reminders (and for this reason *only*).

2. Post on your fridge the number of a florist.

3. If he has an assistant, e-mail him or her important dates.

4. Leave clues around, like pages of a magazine. Be obvious!

5. Tell a friend of his to tell your guy what you want.

6. Reward him when you get a gift. Be very grateful!

7. Buy him gifts too. Even if guys don't care as much, it will show them what's appropriate.

CHAPTER THIRTY-SEVEN

Celebrate Good Times, and Moan with Us During Bad Times

I'm constantly telling my daughter how proud I am of her. Constantly. Endlessly. Even when she hands me a piece of paper with a scribble on it, I tell her how proud I am of her. She puts on her own underwear? I tell her how proud I am of her. She comes home with sixteen out of twenty on a math test, I tell her how proud I am of her. I know this is good for her self-esteem. When she auditioned for a ballet school and was accepted, I told her (and everyone else) how proud I was of her. And she's super proud of me. She'll go into bookstores and tell sales clerks about her mommy's books! My men . . . well, they never seem all *that* proud of me.

I was once invited to an authors' festival. I invited my writer-boyfriend to come with me. "I'm not going to that. I should get my own invitation," he said. I had to explain that I wanted him there to support *me*. "Plus, I'll have more fun with you there," I added. Still, it was a no-go. He refused to come. He was so wrapped up with his bruised ego that he refused to come even as my date.

My married friend in the insurance business never gets any compliments from her husband for doing a good job at work. "Not only that, my husband will talk about someone else in the same field as me. He'll be like, 'She's so smart and so good at what she does.' And does he acknowledge me? No!"

Another friend says her husband never asks her a "thing about my job or what I work on." (Seriously, she jokes, she could be a prostitute and he would have no clue!) "When I lost my job, you'd think he'd be supportive because he has lost so many of his. But all he said was 'You've got to figure out what to do, because we need a second salary.' I was like, 'Thanks for being so understanding!' Then, when I decided to start my own company, not once did he ask, 'What are you going to call it?' He never asked me once if he could help. And he's never once asked how it's going, and it's going really well!"

One of my smartest friends does lectures at Ivy League universities. "My husband would never ask about it, or how it went. But I know every minor thing that goes on in his office," she says.

One woman I know was very upset one night after learning that the bar she had worked at for seven years was closing. She was distraught over this, to say the least. She liked her job, her co-workers, and the people who frequented the bar. Yes, she was distraught. Now, you could say, it's just a bar, and you can find another bar to work. Actually, that's exactly what her boyfriend said to her. "Get over it. It's just a bar. You can find another bar to work." She stormed out of his place. He didn't get why she was so upset.

No matter how small our problems seem to you, when we're upset, we're upset. Something that upsets us is getting into fights with friends. One of my friends is constantly having issues with her group of gal friends. She goes to her husband for support, but he tells her, "I don't want to hear about it." Another friend says her boyfriend doesn't have a lot of tolerance for her problems. "He wants things to be good all the time."

Sometimes things *are* good, and we want you to be happy for us. I once got into a wicked fight with my boyfriend (does it seem I fight a lot?) after I had just finished a book, which took eighteen months out of my life. As soon as I pushed Send and delivered the manuscript, I called my boyfriend. I was feeling like a million bucks. A huge weight had been lifted off my shoulders. Of course, the first person I was going to call was my boyfriend, the one who should be most proud of me when something nice happens to me. Right? Wrong! When I called and told him the news, he sounded tired and said, "That's good." I was taken aback. Then I ranted, "You should be way more happy for me. Why the hell aren't you acting happy? You should be proud of me. You should want to celebrate. You should suggest we go celebrate!"

Okay, the truth was I had woken him up from a nap. Still, when I called my girlfriends to tell them that I had finally finished my book, they were all so excited and told me how awesome I was. And they all wanted to take me out to celebrate. Which is why sometimes I think I should be dating my girlfriends (except that most of them are already taken and also I like men).

I Just Saved You $200 and Forty-five Minutes of Your Time (Total: $3,600)

"Maybe I'm an idealist," says Freud, "but your partner is also your friend. They need to at least listen when good things happen or when bad things happen. Women need men to listen. They want to feel heard. They want to feel valuable. You have to train men to be active but keep their mouths shut. Shut up and listen! You could even take tape out of a drawer, sit him down in a chair, and bring out the handcuffs." (Is he joking? Who cares? It's a good idea! Getting handcuffs is now on my to-do list.)

CLEVER TACTICS/ADVICE ON RAISING YOUR MAN TO ACHIEVE AT OR ABOVE THE EXPECTED LEVEL

1. Before you tell him the good or bad news, warn him that you need him to be supportive.

2. Be upfront and tell him you want to celebrate!

3. Act like you're proud of yourself, and he'll follow suit.

4. Forward all the e-mails from supportive friends and write, "Isn't that nice of them?"

5. Maybe buy some handcuffs and tape, and do sit him down to listen! (Plus, you could always use the handcuffs for other occasions—ahem—if you know what I mean.)

CHAPTER THIRTY-EIGHT

You Can Book a Tee Time but Not a Reservation?

O kay, what I did was awful. (Again, I'm not always the perfect girlfriend, but I never said I was.) But at the time, it seemed appropriate. It was my birthday, and it was a big one. I decided to treat myself to a little spa getaway. I mentioned it to the man I was seeing, who decided to come along. I was excited. I liked this guy. We were supposed to stay three nights. He ended up staying one. Why? Because I kicked him out. Yes, I kicked him out.

What had been going through my head was this: It was my birthday weekend. On our first night there, I called the concierge to see if we could eat at the restaurant. They were booked up until 10:30 p.m. I told my boyfriend this and he said, "Well, call the concierge again and ask him for other places. I'm going to take a shower." I was angry. Why? I thought that he should have taken charge. Or rather, it would have been *nice* if he had taken charge. After all, I had booked the hotel, booked our plane tickets, picked the dates. So why couldn't he pick up the damn phone and call the concierge himself?

Other women I've talked with also complain that their husbands or boyfriends never plan anything. My friend says, "My boyfriend will be like, 'What do you feel like doing tonight?' I'll say, 'I'm up for anything.' And then he'll say, 'Well, like what?' And I'll say, 'ANYTHING,' and he'll be like, 'I don't know. What do you feel like doing?' It's not that he's doing it for me; it's just that he's too damn lazy to think of something, even to suggest going to a movie or picking out a restaurant."

Another married friend seconds this. "He never plans anything. There would be months upon months that we didn't go out. I just want him to say, 'Let's go out for dinner or a movie.' Just the suggestion of it would be nice. We only go out if I say, 'Let's go out.' I am always saying, 'It would be really nice if, once in a while, you could make plans for us. Or you could suggest we go away for a night or go on a day trip.'"

My friend quit. Literally, she just gave up. Even when her in-laws bought her and her husband a trip for his fortieth birthday, it was clear he wouldn't be doing anything. "I'd nag him and nag him to look at airline tickets and hotels. But he couldn't be bothered. So I gave up," she said.

Another woman I know loves almost everything about her boyfriend of a year and a half. She loves how he's so laid back. But she also hates that he's so laid back. "He's so laid back that we never go anywhere. If I don't say we're doing something, we won't do anything. He never makes any plans. Everything has to be spontaneous, and not in a good way. We'll be driving and I'll suggest we go see a play. Of course, you can't get tickets to a play two minutes before it starts. So we end up just driving around."

GUEST APPEARANCE FROM A
REAL-LIFE EX OF MINE!

"Men are hunters and pursuers," said one of my former boyfriends. "But when you get married, it's like women who have a biological clock. A lot of married men just end up sitting watching television. The pursuit is gone. They're married or in a serious relationship. Why should they have to work at planning something? Why don't men take the initiative? Well, it's a long, dark, deep, and complicated [question] . . ." (This is where I cut him off. He's full of shit.)

CLEVER TACTICS/ADVICE ON RAISING YOUR MAN TO ACHIEVE AT OR ABOVE THE EXPECTED LEVEL

1. Don't give up! Suggest it would be nice to go someplace. Ask if he really only wants to watch television for the rest of his life?

2. Leave brochures around the house.

3. Think about if you *really* want him to take the initiative. Remember, you may end up in some shitty hotel.

4. Tell him you're going away yourself. That should get him off his ass and at least spark a discussion.

CHAPTER THIRTY-NINE

Getting High
and Other Bad Habits.
Don't Be a Dope!

I'm shocked at the number of my married friends who, once they put their kids to bed, go out to their garages and backyards and smoke pot. (I don't dare ask, "What came first, the pot smoking or the marriage?") I'm not here to play judge and jury to my friends. It's their lives.

One friend likes to smoke up with her husband occasionally before they go to bed. He likes to smoke up more than she does. "It would drive me nuts when we had arranged a play date and he'd disappear with the other father. And he'd always make arrangements to pick up at the worst times, like bedtime for the children."

Another friend says, "I have to tell him, 'You're not walking into this wedding reeking of pot, with red eyes, because my grandmother wouldn't really appreciate that.'"

"I don't really care that he smokes it," says another woman I know, "but I'm like, 'Can you at least maybe wait until my parents leave?'"

But there are other bad habits. One of my friends complains that her husband never trims DOWN THERE. "So I stopped giving him blow jobs." Another complains that her husband doesn't exercise enough and has stopped giving a "shit" about his appearance. "You'd think you'd want to look your best." Another complains that her husband never goes to the dentist. "It's gross. So I had to make his appointments for him."

I Just Saved You $200 and Forty-five Minutes of Your Time (Total: $3,800)

Freud does not like pot smokers. He makes this loud and clear. "It's the ultimate in hypocrisy. I can't tell you how many sixteen- and seventeen-year-olds I get in here because their parents caught them smoking pot. Guess what? Nine out of ten times, when I ask where they got it, they say it was their parents' stash, or their siblings got it from their parents' stash and gave it to them."

When it comes to other bad habits, though, like the boyfriend of mine who constantly forgot to put on deodorant, Freud says that you have to be their friend and tell them that they smell. "Because you *are* their friend," he repeats.

WISE WORDS FROM HELENA.
She Does My Brazilian Bikini Waxes. She Knows, Hears, and Sees It All!
"My husband bites his nails. And I do manicures for a living!
It bothers the shit out of me. But he's trying. He's trying."
(See how generous Helena can be? And at least he's not smoking dope!)

CLEVER TACTICS/ADVICE ON RAISING YOUR MAN
TO ACHIEVE AT OR ABOVE THE EXPECTED LEVEL

1. Let them have some fun. But tell them there's a time and place for everything.

2. Be patient. Bad habits are hard to break.

3. Be a friend. Gently say, "I like when you smell good. It turns me on."

4. We have bad habits too, don't we? Do they nag us about them?

CHAPTER FORTY

Five Hundred Channels and One Argument

O kay, there are certain shows that definitely fall under the girlie category. These include *The Real Housewives, Gossip Girl, Dancing with the Stars, American Idol,* to name a few. Now, I like these shows. I like them a lot. I like when my boyfriends watch these shows with me, because . . . well, I just like when they watch them with me. I was dating this one guy, and when I was at his house flipping through the channels I ended up on a rerun of *Friends.* "I can't watch this," he said, changing the channel to two dwarfs hitting each other with baseball bats. "I can't watch this!" I moaned, disgusted, grabbing the channel changer and putting it back on *Friends.* We had compromises. We both liked *Celebrity Apprentice* and we both liked *Survivor,* but there was no middle ground for any other show. I told him I liked it when he watched beside me, but he refused. He would go on his computer, putter around, lift weights, and clean his fridge—basically doing anything to not watch with me. "Well, you don't watch sports with me," he said. True. But I argued that he didn't *care* if I watched sports with him. I *cared* that he didn't want to watch *Dancing with the Stars* with me. It's a double standard, I know. But still. There are a lot of double standards when it comes to boys and girls.

Good thing I had PVR at my house, so I could record the shows and watch them later. "There's nothing more annoying than my husband yelling at me, 'Why are you watching this shit?' And I'll be like, 'Because I like *Project Runway.*' I wish he wouldn't stay beside me because he ends up yelling at the television, and then I'll yell at him to go watch his own television. This is why we purposely got two televisions with two PVRs—so we could watch our own shows," one of my friends says.

In this day and age, it's very rare to find a household with only one television. But they do exist. And too bad for those couples, because then the fights over television become even worse, and they're not even about what to watch. Mainly, the fights become about getting another television. "I begged for one in the living room. My husband is anti-television, and I used to be. But I'm not now. We have one in the basement for the children, but I don't want to go down there because it's not relaxing to watch television with toys everywhere," says one woman I know.

Women have other issues surrounding the television. One of my friends is constantly getting pissed off at her boyfriend because he always falls asleep in front of the television. "He'll get in so much trouble," she says. "He'll come up and 6 a.m. and I'll ask what he was doing. He'll say, 'I fell asleep in front of the television again.' It hurts my feelings. It's like he forgets he has a girlfriend waiting for him in bed, and he'd rather sleep on an uncomfortable couch watching infomercials. And of course, don't even ask if I got some. Obviously, I didn't."

A Word from a Grade-A Husband . . .

"If she really, really loves a show, like *The Bachelorette*, and I really, really love her, I'll watch the show. It's as simple as that."

Guest Appearance from a Real-Life Ex of Mine!

"We end up secretly enjoying it more than we admit. If a man sits there and actually watches, he is secretly enjoying it," says one of my exes, who watched *American Idol* with me. "*Sex in the City* was brilliant! But did I make you watch the hockey game with me?" (Moving on . . .)

CLEVER TACTICS/ADVICE ON RAISING YOUR MAN TO ACHIEVE AT OR ABOVE THE EXPECTED LEVEL

1. Tell him you understand that he doesn't like watching what you do, but you like being near him. Cuddle with him, rub his arm, balance out the pain for him of watching the show he hates with some love.

2. Buy junk food. My sister-in-law buys my brother's favourite junk food for him. He will sit and watch anything with her with his favourite dill pickle potato chips.

3. Remind him that the show is only twenty-two minutes of his life. Surely, if he *loves* you, he can spend those twenty-two minutes with you.

4. Maybe you don't want him to watch with you. Is it that important to you? I know a lot of women who would rather their men not watch so they don't have to listen to their comments during the show.

5. Occasionally, watch something he wants. Remember the time and place of his sports game. Tell him he owes you now.

CHAPTER FORTY-ONE

The Adult Temper Tantrum. You Need a Time Out, Mister!

W ith some boyfriends, I was scared to find out their mood at the end of their workday. This is because many, many, many men come home in a foul mood. I get it. Most work at offices. They work hard in competitive, stressful environments. They have to deal with traffic on the way home. They're tired. When my daughter comes home in a bad mood, I know it's most likely because she's exhausted. So I leave her alone. In Parent Land, this is called giving a time out. She needs time just to sit there, unwind, and relax. But many women don't let their husbands do this. I don't let my boyfriends do this. When they are curt to me, I end up yelling, "Tell me what the fuck is wrong with you or lighten the fuck up!" (But I would never yell that at my daughter!)

It's taken a lot of my girlfriends time to realize that there's the Work

HOW IT GOES WITH MY SIX-YEAR-OLD...

"I know you wanted that toy, but it was a stupid toy," I'll say.

"But I really, really wanted it," she'll cry. "It's not fair."

"Life's not fair. Why are you crying?"

"Because I really wanted that toy and you wouldn't let me have it," she'll sob.

"It was a stupid toy. And we're at home now. So forget about it."

"I'm not talking to you," she'll say. (I know. OUCH!)

"I'm not talking to you either," I'll say. Rowan starts crying even harder.

"I think you need a time out. Go to your room and come back down when you've calmed down," I'll tell her.

(And guess what? She does go to her room, and within five minutes, she comes back down and we're talking again like nothing happened!)

Husband who needs time to transform back into the Home Husband. "He'd get aggravated if I had to work late," says one friend. "He'd say, 'Can you go to another room? I can hear you typing too loud. I'm trying to watch television.' He'd get pissed off if he had to be a parent. I'm like, 'I'm not just twiddling my fingers fourteen hours a day.'"

I Just Saved You $200 and Forty-five Minutes of Your Time (Total: $4,000)

Sometimes I don't like Freud. Today is one of those days, and I tell him so. "I don't like you," I say. I had asked him what a woman can do when her guy is in a bad mood. His answer was "Actually, women tend to be more moody." Thanks for that, buddy! I wasn't asking that. "I was asking you what a woman can do when her partner comes home in a bad mood," I say to Freud. He suggests avoidance. Hmmm. Interesting. "Give them space. And tell them that you're giving them space to sort out their feelings. Say it with love." However, Freud says, if it becomes a routine and your man is coming home in a bad mood every single day, you must stick up for yourself and set limits. He says you can say, "Don't take your bad mood out on me." But you must also always ask, "What can I do to help?"

Guest Appearance from a Real-Life Ex of Mine!

So why do men have adult temper tantrums? I asked an ex who was prone to this. I also asked what women can do when men have them. (I couldn't do anything right. I made his temper tantrums *worse.*) "Men are children. What you *don't* do is tell us that you love us when we're in the middle of our rants with that special little voice that women have. It makes us enraged. It's not what you *can* do when we have our tantrum; it's what you *don't* do that matters. You don't walk away, you don't show affection or tell us you love us, you don't try to help us. But at the same time, we don't want to be left alone. It's a common misconception that we want sympathy. We don't. We want our girlfriends there, but we don't want any huffiness or any reaction. And *do not* ask how you can help. Never, ever ask!" (Gee, can you see why *men* are so hard to live with?)

CLEVER TACTICS/ADVICE ON RAISING YOUR MAN TO ACHIEVE AT OR ABOVE THE EXPECTED LEVEL

1. Let him rant, but only to a point. I say ten minutes is reasonable to just listen. (This is based on experience with my daughter; her tantrums never lasted longer.)
2. After you let him rant for an acceptable amount of time, leave the room and say you're upstairs if he needs you.
3. Get into a hot shower. You'll enjoy it, and you won't be able to hear him.
4. Realize it is not about you. So *do not* blame yourself. In fact, try to enjoy yourself during these tantrums. Daydream about a sunny beach or use the time wisely thinking about the things you need to get done.
5. Buy earplugs. Seriously, there are some really good earplugs out there that others can't even notice are in your ears.

CHAPTER FORTY-TWO

How to Travel Together. It's NOT a Day at the Spa

———◆———

Travelling is a really good way of figuring out if you're compatible with someone. "It's like my husband is in competition with himself to see how little he can pack for a trip," my married friend moans. "We'll be going away for a week and he'll pack, like, two pairs of underwear. I'm like, 'This is not cute. This is not funny. This is gross.'"

Another woman travelled with her boyfriend of eight months. "He ran out of money. He took enough cash for two days and that was it. I'm like, 'We're here for eight days!' I had to explain to him how to wire money. He really had no idea how much money he would need to travel."

I once went away with a man to a sunny destination. I knew that it was a mistake, that we were incompatible travellers, when he lay by the pool and asked for some specialized suntan lotion. It was so specialized that I wondered why he didn't plan in advance and pick it up before he came. Travel, to me, is very important. I can't be with a man who does not like to travel. Once I arranged a trip for my boyfriend and me, and we were going to meet at the airport at our destination. "So what do we do then?" he asked. "How do we get to the hotel?" I said, "Well, there are two ways: you take a damn taxi or you call the hotel to pick you up." Obviously, at thirty-nine years old, he hadn't travelled at all.

Other women moan that they just want to lie on a beach and read. One of my friends complains that she needs a vacation after her vacation because her husband is an "active" traveller. That means he can't sit still, let alone lie on a beach, for more than five minutes. "We always have to be doing something. I'm like, 'Please, can you just let me read?'"

Most of my friends will say that a couple who can't travel together probably shouldn't be together. That's why a lot of them break up with their sort-of boyfriends early. "I went to New York after three weeks dating a guy," a friend says. "I realized we were just so incompatible. He wanted to go to punk rock shows late at night, and I wanted to go to plays. When we got back, we never spoke again."

Another couple I know are also not compatible when it comes to travelling together. "I go on vacation basically to detox," she says. "What I mean is that I want to eat healthy, I want to get a lot of sleep, I want to exercise. But my husband just wants to party late at night, because that's what vacation is to him."

GUEST APPEARANCE FROM A
REAL-LIFE EX OF MINE!

One ex of mine spent a lot of time in another country. Lucky fuck. Anyway, I would meet him sometimes for a few days here and there, though we never were on the same plane together. He liked to party and go to bars at night, while, after a day at the beach, I wanted to be in bed by nine. To give credit where credit is due, he was good about this. Shockingly, he has some very interesting thoughts for couples who travel together. "You can tell everything about a relationship by whether your girlfriend will take the middle seat on an airplane. The guy always wants the window or aisle. If a girl doesn't sit in the middle and insists the man does, the vacation will not be good. The best thing for a girl to do in a relationship is take the middle seat." He also has some . . . um, interesting thoughts for couples who don't like to do the same thing on vacations. "I'd say tell the women to get a prescription for anti-anxiety drugs and just go along for the ride. In my experience, travelling together is like speed-dialling the relationship. I like to travel, and if the person I'm dating doesn't like to do what I do, then I know the relationship won't last."

CLEVER TACTICS/ADVICE ON RAISING YOUR MAN TO ACHIEVE AT OR ABOVE THE EXPECTED LEVEL

1. If you know you're not compatible travelling, make the trip shorter than longer. Three days max.

2. Tell him this time you want a beach vacation. Next time, you'll go on the bike trip excursion.

3. Go away with a girlfriend instead. I do this.

4. Think about vacationing with another couple. It will take the pressure off if your man has another man to do "active" stuff with (while you spend the day at the spa with your girlfriend).

CHAPTER FORTY-THREE

Money, Money, Honey . . .

———◆———

P eople are funny about money. Most of my friends who date will share the bill, but honestly, they'd prefer it if the guy paid. "I went on a date and I offered to pay half. But he wasn't doing anything. It looked like he wasn't even going to pay his half. So I went to the bathroom and just left. I figured taking a taxi home would be cheaper than paying anyway." See? See what we women will do when we really believe in something? Another man this same woman dated took her to a very fancy restaurant. When the bill came, he asked if they took Interac. "They looked at him like he was crazy. It was this fancy French restaurant, and he's asking if he could use his bank card. So then he says, 'Okay, I'll just run to a bank machine.' All the red flags went up at that point. That was totally classless. If you're going on a date, maybe you should make sure you have money in your wallet first!"

A lot of women sneak in clothes. I've done it. "He had no problem spending money on poker nights with his friends, but when it came to me saying, 'Let's go out for a nice dinner,' he'd say, 'I don't want to spend the money.' He always complained about money. If I bought something, he'd be like, 'Because you needed another pair of shoes.' And I'd be like, 'Yeah, I did. I paid my portion of this month's bills.'"

One of my friends is rich. Her husband is rich too. But for some reason, she always ends up paying for everything that has to do with their three children. I suggested she invoice him. "I do," she says. "Every month, I give him a detailed list of what our bills are and he writes me a check."

Seriously. Are marriages now business transactions?

———◆———

I Just Saved You $200 and Forty-five Minutes of Your Time (Total: $4,200)

"Money and sex are the two most common problems and indicators in a relationship about trust and intimacy. My clients always ask about money and sex. The way money is handled is about trust and power. There are couples in relationships who just have one joint account and they have a basic understanding that you can buy some clothes for a few hundred dollars but not a new car. To me, this shows respect and a balance of power. But then there are couples who each have their own accounts, plus a joint account that they contribute to for joint expenses. If you keep all your money to yourself and he keeps all his money to himself, then you're waiting for a failure."

WISE WORDS FROM HELENA.
She Does My Brazilian Bikini Waxes. She Knows, Hears, and Sees It All!

"My husband is in the construction business, so sometimes he works a lot and then sometimes he can go weeks without working. But my theory is that if you're married, me casa es su casa. *What's mine is yours. I'm old school like that, but it works for us. I love him, and when he's not working, he feels bad enough. We're in this together."*
She is also old school when it comes to dating. "Guys should always pay on the first few dates at the very least. Trust me, we gals will have to pay on other levels."

CLEVER TACTICS/ADVICE ON RAISING YOUR MAN TO ACHIEVE AT OR ABOVE THE EXPECTED LEVEL

1. Split the bill.

2. Discuss money and what your goals are before you get serious.

3. Sneak in clothes (because, honestly, it's easier than fighting about it).

4. Don't make him feel bad if you make more money. Money is an ego thing for most men. Understand this. Know this.

TIME FOR THE RELATIONSHIP
REPORT CARD!
(Feel Free to Mail This to Your Guy!)

Does he demonstrate a positive attitude?

A   B   C   D

Does he have pride in good workmanship?

A   B   C   D

Does he demonstrate logical thinking?

A   B   C   D

Does he obtain information through observation?

A   B   C   D

Does he use information to make predictions?

A   B   C   D

Comments . . .

PART FIVE

I Know This
Is the Way
You Are

———

You Can't Be Raised When It Comes to Certain Things.
But These Are Worth Mentioning in Relationships Because They Are Annoying.

CHAPTER FORTY-FOUR

Snorers,
Yes, You Do So Snore!

I'm always disappointed when I find out after a sleepover that the man I'm dating is a snorer. At first, I don't really mind. The *first* night, I don't mind. After all, I'm just so *happy* to be with a man. But I'm the type of gal who needs eight hours of sleep to function. And it may just be my bad luck, but I've *never* been with a guy who doesn't snore. I've also never been with a guy who admits he snores (even though they all do).

I know sleeping over brings couples closer, but really, I can't stand snorers. I'm such a light sleeper that I literally can hear my BlackBerry vibrate downstairs, even if my bedroom door is shut. So imagine how I am with a man who sleeps next to me and snores. In the drawer in my nightstand, I have earplugs, nose strips, and even a couple of emergency sleeping pills. This is all for boyfriends who are snorers. I also have a humidifier and a noise machine. Swear to God, I have not been with one man in my entire life who wasn't a snorer. This includes my baby brother, with whom I once had to share a room at the cottage. My parents came in one night to see me suffocating him with a pillow. "He snores! I can't sleep." (Needless to say, my parents gave me my own room after that.)

I'm not the only one who hates snorers. (Does anyone like snorers?) "I have to fall asleep first or I am fucked," says one of my married friends. "I kick him all night long. It wakes him up and he'll scream at me, 'What? You scared the shit out of me!' We'll literally get into a fight about his snoring at 3 a.m. Finally he went to a specialist and he had another follow-up appointment, which he missed, and he never went back again. He cared about his snoring for a week. I can't tell you how many times I end up on the couch, watching bad television until I pass out," she moans.

Now, I realize that you can't raise a non-snorer. But you can raise a snorer who will at least *admit* to being a snorer. One of my married friends doesn't sleep in the same room as her husband. I know this because her three-year-old took me on a tour of their new house and pointed out, "That's my daddy's room. My mommy's room is upstairs." I went back and suggested to my friend that maybe she shouldn't let her son give tours anymore. "He likes pointing out that Mommy and Daddy don't sleep together." My friend too is a light sleeper. Her husband—you guessed it—is a snorer.

The problem with guys is that they never admit they snore. "I don't snore!" they'll say. And I'll say, "Yes, you do. I was up all night listening to you snore!" Truthfully, I just want them to ADMIT they snore. That's it.

CHAPTER FORTY-FIVE

Temperature Rising: Air Conditioner Wars

I wasn't sure if I was alive or dead when I woke up. I was so cold that I thought I had frostbite. My nose was freezing. I couldn't feel my fingers or toes. My ex loved air conditioning. He loved it so much, he'd have it on even during winter. Now, because I have many traits like a senior citizen, I am not comfortable unless the temperature outside (and inside) is at least seventy-five degrees. "You'll sleep better when it's cooler," he'd always tell me. "Yes, because I may be dead I'm so friggin cold."

Most women I know are always more cold then their boyfriends or husbands. When I lived with the father of my daughter, we had a fancy machine that controlled the temperature. He'd like it at sixty-eight degrees. I would like it at seventy-eight degrees. He'd turn it down. I'd turn it up. "Did you turn it up again?" he'd ask. Of course I lied. He got furious at the fancy machine, which he said he couldn't figure out because it was always going up for no reason. (Yes, it was always going up because I'd been turning it up.) In fact, he actually got a professional to come in to fix the thing, which really wasn't broken at all. In any case, it's hard to live with someone when you're always cold. Especially at night. I'd have to wear layers—*yes, layers*—to get warm and then pile three blankets on. If I did get away with turning up the temperature, he'd be yelling at me, "It's like a spa in here! I'm sweating! How can I sleep like this?" Yeah, well, you think it's comfortable to sleep in layers with piles of blankets on you? Men have hair on their body, so this keeps them warmer, I think. Or generally, they have more body fat.

"I hate air conditioning," agrees one of my friends. "I hate it in the car. I hate it in the house. I honestly think that air conditioning gives me colds." When they drive together and her husband puts on the air conditioning, she'll roll down her window. This is their compromise. Yet neither of them is exactly happy with the compromise.

Usually, I prefer my boyfriends to sleep at my place. (What can I say? My bed is way more comfortable and also I want to wake up in my own house.) Boyfriends sleeping over is very, *very* rare, since I have a daughter. When one of my exes slept over, he complained about how hot it was in my room. I told him the air conditioning was broken, but I'd get it fixed "tomorrow." Did I? Of course not. I like it hot. Deal with it.

No More Pencils, No More Books, No More Boyfriend's Dirty Looks!

S o can you really raise a boyfriend? Can you really raise a husband? Can you really raise *any* man? I can tell you this much: the men I date are dealing with a new (and maybe improved) woman. I've learned a lot throughout this process of meeting and talking to other women. I've learned that, yes, indeed, you can raise a boyfriend or a husband. But like raising a child, this takes patience. I've learned to be more patient when it comes to men. It took patience, after all, to teach my daughter how to read. It took patience to teach her to sleep in her own bed. It takes patience to teach her pretty much everything. Also, it takes a sense of humour to raise a man. I now can laugh at men's sometimes clueless behaviours. And not because if I didn't laugh, I would probably cry. I laugh because their cluelessness, and my cluelessness in how to deal with their cluelessness, *is* funny. Also, I now know that I'm not alone. I'm not the *only* woman out there with clueless men. At certain times, I did wonder why so many women put up with so much shit in relationships. But I also refuse to give up, and I hope other women won't either. I won't give up teaching my daughter to tell time, and I won't give up raising her to one day be a productive member of society. I won't give up teaching my daughter to tie her shoes. So why should I give up raising the men in my life to clean up after themselves or give me a compliment? I've also learned that what's important to women is not always important to men. I now remind myself of this. I've learned too that when you're really in love, and the man is really worth it, you must take the good with the bad And you know what? The bad is not always so bad.

I Just Saved You $200 and Forty-five Minutes of Your Time (Total: $4,400)

Freud is not as optimistic as I am when it comes to raising a boyfriend or a husband, though he thinks, in theory, attempting to do so is wonderful. "Some men are just looking for a mother and a caregiver. And some women find themselves falling into that role. Both women and men need to know that there is a difference between the caregiver role and a partnership," says Freud. "And perhaps, some men just can't be raised." Only you can figure out if your man can be raised and is worthy of it.

My good girlfriend says that men can be raised, *except* when it comes to "bottom lines." Everyone in a relationship has "bottom lines." Is it a bottom line for you if a guy doesn't say thank you? Maybe not. But if he doesn't say thank you and he doesn't compliment you and he's always late and he bails on you all the time, maybe that's your bottom line.

There *are* certain circumstances in which a man can, and will, never be raised. And it's better you find this stuff out earlier than later. I'll give you an example. My thirty-five-year-old friend had been seeing a man for almost ten weeks. They were out for dinner one night when he suddenly said to her, "We've never discussed this, but I never want to be married again and I don't want any more children." My friend dropped her fork and said, "Okay, this dinner is over." She told him never to call her again. She wanted to get married. She wanted to have children. That was her bottom line. You can't raise a man who is so positive that he doesn't want those things if that's his bottom line.

Even if men don't like the idea of being raised, they can at least admit that it isn't the worst idea in the world. "Of course a man can be raised just like a child. That's what women are there for. It's not an easy process. In fact, it can be really difficult. But men definitely do get raised. Left on their own, they'd be wolves," says one of my exes.

As Helena puts it: "They can be raised, but maybe only to a certain extent. You can raise them to be not so rough around the edges. And hopefully, by the time you do raise them, you'll still want them."

After talking and thinking for months about relationships—the good, the bad, the ugly—I still keep coming back to the same conclusion: that everything that is taught can be learned. One just needs patience. And know this: report cards do not come just once a year. There are usually three terms in every school year, so there are three report cards. Be patient. Raising a boyfriend is a process. Perhaps by the third term, after a few months, your man will surprise you with what he's learned and how much he's grown. You may be surprised too at what a good teacher you have become. You may re-read this book and find that your answers and comments have changed. How exciting would that be?

Right now, I've got to go. I've got to tell my daughter she can't skateboard in the house. And then I have to go call my boyfriend. My daughter is definitely worth raising. And this time, I think, this boyfriend is too. I'm an optimist. Everything that is taught can be learned. And I've done a friggin fantastic job with my daughter, if I do say so myself. And I'm her role model. I just know that by the time she starts dating, the man in my life will be consistently achieving at or above the expected level. I expect no less for me, and certainly no less for my daughter.

In the process of writing this book, I was dating someone seriously. He needed a lot of raising, which I tirelessly attempted. (He gave me a lot of material.) He had his good qualities. He could cook and, um . . . well he could cook really, really, really well. Although I am very competitive, and hate to admit defeat, I just couldn't "Raise" him. He was a never-ending problem Adult Child, who just couldn't live up to my standards of parenting. (He stayed at a constant "D" on the Relationship Report Card.) I chose to concentrate on continuing to raise my daughter and throw him back into the dating world, where another woman will either a) have to raise him or b) overlook what I perceived to be major character flaws in an adult male, or c) maybe (hopefully) he did LEARN a few things from me and in his next relationship he'll be a little more "raised." (If you're dating him now, you can thank me later.)

Though we are no longer together (pause for tiny violin) and there was heartbreak, I realized this was not necessarily a bad thing. After a couple of weeks, I realized that it WAS easier to raise a child, than raise a child AND a man. I felt a huge amount of stress vanish. A mere three weeks later I was introduced to a man in his late 30s, divorced, with two children. Although we've only recently started dating he always opens doors, listens to my stories, compliments me, and, so far, has always been punctual. Once when he was going to be five minutes late, he called to let me know that he was going to be five minutes late. And he was only five minutes late.

I'm not scared when he's driving and he makes dinner reservations for us. Of course, this could be because he's on his best behavior in these early stages of dating. I'm sure I will find out soon enough that there are some area(s) in which he needs to be raised. But this man also has two young daughters.

Perhaps because he's raising children he, too, has certain expectations for how human beings should and shouldn't act. Perhaps he's treating me the way he'd like his daughters to be treated when they start dating. The true sign of a successful relationship will come the day I go grocery shopping with another man again. I eagerly await the day.

Thanks to my exes who are still speaking to me, I learned a lot about myself in the process of writing this book. My god, I can be annoying and demanding! Interviewing other women, married and in serious relationships, I realized that we females DO have high expectations. I'm not saying it's wrong to, it's just that I realized that sometimes I'm the one who just need to let things go. Not everything, but definitely some things. I also find that the happier I am with myself, the less I need phone calls or compliments. That's not to say I don't want them, and that men shouldn't give them, but I'm less aware when I'm not getting them.

I've definitely learned that I was clueless—and sometimes just plain bitchy—in the way I went about getting what I wanted and needed out of a relationship. I'm not as clueless now. I'm certainly not as bitchy.

I always come back to: is this man treating me like I'd like my daughter to be treated in a relationship? I don't expect perfection but I do expect common courtesy and civility, as should you. I wish you all the best in "raising" your boyfriend or any other clueless guy in your life. It's not easy, but then again, who said parenting was?

Acknowledgments

———

T hank you to Kristin Cochrane, Amy Black and Lynn Henry, all who "got" the idea for this book instantly. Thank you for the laughs during the initial meeting. More kudos to Amy for her enviable editing skills, ideas, and for making the process of this book FUN from start to finish! Thanks, too, to Scott Sellers, who—what can I say?—J'adore! Thank you to Scott Richardson who did an amazing job with the design. And thank you to Suzanne Brandreth, my agent.

I REALLY have to thank the women in my family, my mother and sister-in-law, Jacqueline, who have listened to me cry, many, many times over men. I love you.

My gal pals, Rebecca, Jasmine, Liza, Joanna, Carolynn, Victoria, Kate, Dianne, and Erica: Thank you for never getting tired of me moaning and always giving me pep talks. My friends are nothing short of amazing. And thanks to Helena Martinez, my wonderfully optimistic aesthetician, who makes me laugh more than cry!

I also have to thank my exes. You were not ALWAYS wrong. I'd regret not mentioning that. And to the wonderful women in this book who were more than willing to share their horror stories: thank you for making me laugh until I cried.

Thank you to Ken Whyte and Pamela Wallin, my mentors always. And to SJC who, for better and/or worse, always has my back. I am appreciative and grateful.